Success, Substance,
and Significance

Success, Substance, and Significance

Gateways to More Giving, Living, and Greater Destiny

Jack C. McDowell

© 2017 Jack C. McDowell
All rights reserved.

ISBN-13: 9781927961094
ISBN-10: 1927961092

Table of Contents

Foreword vii
Introduction ix

PART ONE: DO THE BEST YOU CAN 1
Chapter 1   More Success, Substance, and Significance 3
Chapter 2   The Desired Destiny 12
Chapter 3   The Power of Your Mind 19
Chapter 4   Dreams and Visions 26
Chapter 5   Body and Soul 38
Chapter 6   Our Endless Spirit 47
Chapter 7   The Greatest Life Insurance 56

PART TWO: WITH WHAT YOU HAVE 67
Chapter 8   The Assets You Possess 69
Chapter 9   The Power of Vision 77
Chapter 10 The Right Attitude 85
Chapter 11 Think! 91
Chapter 12 Expectations and Opportunities 100

PART THREE: WHERE YOU ARE 111
Chapter 13 Where You Are 113
Chapter 14 What We Believe 122
Chapter 15 When We Take the Initiative 134
Chapter 16 Financial Freedom 143

Chapter 17 Honest Effort · 154
Chapter 18 Our Place ·163
Chapter 19 Person to Person ·173

PART FOUR: AT ALL TIMES. 185
Chapter 20 Seasons and Echoes of Life · · · · · · · · · · · · · · · ·187
Chapter 21 The Honest Truth ·197
Chapter 22 Obstacles and Barriers · · · · · · · · · · · · · · · · · · · 208
Chapter 23 Respect and Honor · 223
Chapter 24 Be Strong and Courageous · · · · · · · · · · · · · · · 233
Chapter 25 Gateways to Purpose and Significance · · · · · · · · ·247
Chapter 26 A Walk with an Older Man · · · · · · · · · · · · · · · · 259

About the Author · 265

Foreword

As you read *Success, Substance, and Significance*, you come to know the merciful, forgiving, and idealistic beliefs of Jack C. McDowell. His values ring true because they work. Not only has this one man exhibited the rugged spirit and strong beliefs for which Americans are celebrated, but his lengthy experience in career and post-career work has exhibited astounding success.

Readers will see that the lives they most admire are those of individuals not primarily seeking success and substantial reward, though those are commendable, but souls who understand the significance of each stage of their lives, their revealed purpose, and their smallest actions.

Jack illustrates his chapters with stories of many interesting people of every age, class, and background. His remarkable insights into how one person after another discovers his or her destiny speaks to the heart of the author, who understands we are all one, each created for a divine time and purpose.

Success, Substance, and Significance encourages us to do what we can to love one another, to be merciful, but above all to be forgiving. That opens all the possibilities to make every day matter, every word and deed matter, but blessedly to accept who we are, where we are, and to rejoice together.

Jack's writing shows the way. His soul is at peace, and rightly so. Read *Success, Substance, and Significance* and recognize the unique significance of your own destiny.

James B. Miller, Jr.
Chairman, Fidelity Southern Corporation
Atlanta, Georgia

Introduction

YOU CAN DO whatever you desire to do, if you will prepare yourself to accept the responsibility involved. You can be what you desire to be, if you will commit yourself in mind and soul to the objective you hope to achieve. If you will do the best you can with what you have, you will be as successful as you are capable of being. When you are successful you must be willing to share your success. Gratitude and generosity are essential to a meaningful and fulfilling life. When you build your purpose on noble principles, and work for worthy causes, your life becomes an example worth following. Love others as you would have them love you. Let the power of your purpose establish the value of your life.

America was founded upon the principle of equal opportunity and the values of individual resourcefulness and freedom of choice. It was this dream of opportunity that inspired the purpose of my life. I had little when I began and nothing of material worth, but I had a vision that I would follow and a God in whom I believed. I educated myself in the use of my talents and created the ability to use them wisely and honestly for the benefit of others.

To dream dreams and have visions is wonderful, but without a purpose and the commitment to fulfill the purpose, all is lost through sublimation and procrastination. The meaning of the American Dream, is the opportunity it offers those who are willing to do their best, with what they have, where they are, at all times. It is freedom of opportunity, freedom to work, and freedom to believe in what we believe.

Part One: Do the Best You Can

"Do your best when no one is looking. If you do that, then you can be successful in anything that you put your mind to."

BOB COUSY

CHAPTER 1

More Success, Substance, and Significance

THIS PRAYER THAT guided my life may help guide yours: **"Dear Father, help me to do the best I can, with what I have, where I am, at all times."** I believe this four-step plan will guarantee any individual anywhere, at any stage of their life, more success, more substance, and more significance. This four-step plan has proven its value among individuals of every race, creed, and culture. This plan might be considered by some outdated or simplistic in today's rapidly changing world, where most things seem to move at lightning speed, without considering the personal qualities of character that make life worth living. Few actually consider how this comprehensive plan encompasses all that we can do with the talents and abilities we possess. Ask yourself if anyone has ever suggested this simple strategy to you:

- *Do the best you can*
- *With what you have*
- *Where you are*
- *At all times*

Life coaches and career consultants generally urge individuals to enhance their major talents, ignore personal weaknesses, or designate minor tasks to others. There is merit in this, as any Olympic athlete knows. It is important that we train our strengths and respect our talents, but many successful individuals who at some point in their lives lose everything, attribute their personal failures to overlooking a lesser but necessary part of their life. Conversely, our four-step plan could be dismissed as advocating far too much effort concerning lesser tasks or minor aspects of their life. As we will show you, this four-step plan has proven itself millions of times throughout the world's history among individuals of every era and every circumstance.

Our success comes in increments throughout the various stages of our life. Today's neuroscience, by mapping actions of the human brain, can show exactly how a thought, decision, word, or emotion can affect the brain and its influences on every part of the body. Our mind directs our brain, which directs our body. Our decision to do our best generates success in every decision or action we take. We decide to pay our bill the day it arrives, to do our holiday shopping early, to plan our week and work our plan, and so forth. Science tells us that each successful effort creates dopamine and serotonin, which provide a state of well-being within the brain. Neglected tasks or jobs poorly done create confusion in our brains that are toxic. Each indecision, incomplete job, or ill-spoken word we wish we could retrieve are costly to our mental and emotional efficiency.

The simple decision to do our best enables us to become more productive and more successful each day. The freedom of thought this decision creates gives us peace of mind and the positive attitude we need to combat the problems and unexpected circumstances we face daily. This mindset introduces us to our positive thought flow which generates our mental creativity. As we attempt to succeed in whatever we say or do, we lift our mind and thoughts to an ever-higher level, because of the faith we have in the value of our efforts.

Ask yourself what is the one thing most likely to block your success? No matter how well our life is going now, most of us have a nagging feeling that something is lacking in our life. An honest evaluation will usually indicate the problem we face that we'd rather ignore:

- *The need to improve personal relationships?*
- *The need to do more for the benefit of others?*
- *The need to more adequately fulfill our commitments?*
- *The need to prepare ourselves more thoroughly for the problems we face?*
- *The need to focus our thoughts more effectively?*

Such questions are commonplace and can be adequately answered. Think of how you can do your best to improve yourself. You will be surprised at how readily others in your life will help when you show your appreciation. Sincere attention and committed efforts produce daily achievements and success.

The amount of substance in any person's life lies in the eyes of the beholder. Many wealthy people never feel they have enough, regardless of how much they have. Many people who live in poverty believe there is no way they will ever have enough. The truth is that anyone who is willing to do their best will significantly increase their substance, and the tangible and intangible values of their life. To do one's best is to become one's best.

In the 38 years I served as The Salvation Army Management Counsel, I guided thousands of America's top CEOs and community leaders in efforts to reach a civic goal—building educational facilities, hospitals, colleges, and churches, and several other lasting, beneficial facilities. I found myself exposed to some of the most brilliant minds and admirable characters anyone could be fortunate enough to know. Most of their success secrets and work ethics were very much the same, but within their personal lives I discovered great variations.

I recall one highly successful CEO who thanked me for selecting him to serve as chairman of a large, multimillion-dollar project. Though successful and wealthy, possessing everything he could possibly want, his life was lacking one thing: he had never experienced the joy of creating something of enduring benefit for the welfare of those far less privileged than himself. This gentleman's work ethic had provided far more substance in terms of possessions, influence, recognition, and pleasures than most families will ever enjoy. Yet he lacked personal knowledge of the intangible substance that is the only thing that really matters. His unpaid work and genuine commitment to a worthy project that benefited his community, gave this man's life a new meaning far beyond anything his money and power had ever provided.

Yes, your life should increase in substance and value year after year as long as you live. Your lands, possessions, business, and money in the bank, accrue slowly but consistently as you plan for them to increase through your worthy and honorable efforts. By doing our best and becoming our best, the substance of our character, our mind, and our personality constantly increases. A substantial reputation is one of honesty, truthfulness, integrity, dependability, and promises kept.

Every child should be encouraged to begin as soon as possible to build his or her character and good reputation. Every adult who has diminished his or her life through thoughtless words and acts can rebuild a desired life, if they are willing to do the best they can with what they have. We all know individuals who make grievous mistakes and believe they have lost everything. That is never true. This four-step plan will help anyone redeem past mistakes and rebuild character flaws of every kind. As many learn, God is the God of second chances and rebuilt lives.

Our life's significance goes far beyond the effect of our personal success. As a stone thrown into still water produces ripples, each ripple touching the next, perhaps extending as far as the eye can see, so our life touches the lives of others and influences them for generations to come. None of us knows how much influence our life exerts on the lives it touches. A little-known evangelist preached to small towns in tent meetings for years. His name was little known and his words hardly remembered, but his message reached one North Carolina farm boy and changed his life. That boy was inspired to study to become an evangelist and, as everyone knows, Billy Graham has preached the gospel to millions of people in more countries than anyone before in history. No school teacher, politician, military officer, or parent will ever know the influence of words they used which will ignite a person who became a torch-bearer for his or her generation.

If doing your best is important, as each of us knows it is, our best words and our best actions carry far more importance and endure far longer than any manmade edifice or creation. Think of the words that have inspired or encouraged you. Ask yourself whether your words criticize, mock, or condemn others, or whether they encourage, edify, and perhaps even inspire others. The significance of your words, your ideas, and your attitudes cannot be overstated. They are your legacy which will live in the memories of those who have known you.

With this quick overview of the reason we should build our life, our substance, and increase our significance for the benefit of others, it's easy to see there are too many benefits to list them separately. To do the best we can, with what we have, where we are, has always been extolled by far too many people to list. One of these was President Theodore Roosevelt, a commanding figure, famous for suggesting we "Speak softly but carry a big stick." More to our point, however, Roosevelt also advised:

"DO WHAT YOU CAN, WITH WHAT YOU HAVE, WHERE YOU ARE."

His successful decisions during the Spanish-American War showed a man of great vigor and influence, a man who expected his nation to flourish. If this plan produced prosperity many times in history, it has guaranteed its own survival. Millions of families successfully survived the Great Depression, as each member did their best with what they had where they were.

Betty Jean Robinson, well-known singer, songwriter, and television host, grew up in Appalachia during that time. In her book, *Up on Melody Mountain*, she tells how her family enjoyed working a garden and raising chickens. She describes turning the earth with her favorite hoe and sharpening the tool with a special rock. She jokes that nothing was wasted ever: using cardboard in their shoes to cover the holes in their soles, papering the log cabin walls with newspapers, and reutilizing "…a piece of fatback, first cooked down in a pot of beans, and then used to grease some tools…"

My wife Peggy and I have traveled to 110 countries over the past five decades. Everything we have seen and learned from these widely differing countries and cultures makes me understand that humans are far more similar than we are different. We have seen countless ways people do their best with what they have, marveling at their ingenuity and the desire to improve their lives. This spirit resides in each of us to some degree, although affluence and luxury can dull the need for ingenuity and decrease enthusiasm and creativity. When we become acquainted with our most basic needs, those necessary to nurture the humanity in every person, we grow in intellect and ability. By doing our best we become the person we are capable of being. We become a person who can help those who come within the sphere of our influence, and at times those far from us.

Think about President Abraham Lincoln. His parents married, had three children, and worked on various farms in Kentucky and Indiana. The first two children, Sarah and Abraham, survived, but the third did not. Abraham helped his father build a log cabin for the family. He was nine years old when his mother, Nancy Hanks Lincoln, died. Unable to attend school, Lincoln worked at any odd jobs he could find. His sister encouraged him to educate himself; eventually he would walk five miles to borrow a law book, return home, and study by firelight. By doing his best in all circumstances, the young man finally became qualified to practice law. But then his business partnerships failed, and he spent years repaying his debts. He lost five elections before becoming President of the United States during the lowest point in his Nation's history, a time when the Union was dissolving.

President Abraham Lincoln, by dint of utilizing every part of our four-point plan, persevered through national and personal tragedy to the successful conclusion of a bitter and costly war, and helped reconcile and unify our Nation and abolish slavery. The significance of this one man's tragic and sorrowful life has existed through the decades and exerts its influence even today. Lincoln could never have imagined the ultimate significance of his decisions, examples, and his lifetime legacy.

Countless other human lives parallel that of Lincoln's. Such people never appeared to have the opportunity or chance to succeed. I was one of these people. I had two loving parents who gave me all they could, but they had nothing material to give to me. By the time I was 12, my parents' good life had fallen apart. Two years earlier, my father's business partner died in his arms. My father soon lost his prosperous real estate business, his horse farm, and his health during the Great Depression. We moved to Northern Minnesota to an abandoned farm, as I entered my teen years. I learned to do a man's work. There was no opportunity for school, sports, or other boyhood activities. Instead, I watched as my sick father gathered all his resources to care for our family. Our assets included that long-abandoned farm with no electricity, heat, running water, or telephone. I don't remember if my father ever instructed me to do my best with what I had where I was, but his daily instructions dictated that I do so. My father's greatest assets were his devoted wife, an obedient son, and that dilapidated farmhouse. From that beginning, my father showed me how to create a prosperous stock farm during the final years of the Great Depression and the challenging years of World War II.

None of us always feels like doing our best. Milking 25 cows twice a day never aroused real enthusiasm in me, nor did the continuous sawing and chopping of wood for heating and cooking, the endless pails of water I pumped and carried to the house, nor any of the daily chores that never seemed to end. However, I now bless those long, exhausting days that I tried so hard to forget. I bless the character of my parents who showed me that doing my best with what I had wherever I was created the character and habits that enabled me to overcome difficulties, because they showed me that we are built to overcome the problems we face. My life's pattern was based on the lessons they taught me, the kind that outlast the difficulties we face.

Those two people were the ones who gave significance to my life. They were little known, except in the small town of Backus, whereas my life eventually touched and influenced millions of other lives throughout our country. As Abraham Lincoln said about the life that proved most significant to him:

"ALL THAT I AM OR HOPE TO BE, I OWE TO MY ANGEL MOTHER."

The brief life of his mother held little beyond hard work and a pioneering spirit, but her influence on his life changed the history of our nation. We all have such an influence in our own way. While I now recognize how much my demanding but absolutely honest and ethical father had on my life, I can also echo Lincoln's words about my mother. She was the most nearly perfect woman I have ever known.

The fact is, each life, on balance, either diminishes or enhances this world. My decision to do my best began a future and legacy that cannot be measured or imagined. As we examine the benefits of this decision, story after story will demonstrate and hopefully inspire you to do **"The best you can, with what you have, where you are, at all times**," and witness how it increases the significance of your life.

Life is intended to be an exciting and rewarding experience. Our creation is a miracle. We were intended to become all we are capable of being. We were created to fulfill a purpose, and in fulfilling that purpose we fulfill our life.

> *"DO ALL THE GOOD YOU CAN. BY ALL THE MEANS YOU CAN. IN ALL THE WAYS YOU CAN. IN ALL THE PLACES YOU CAN. AT ALL THE TIMES YOU CAN. TO ALL THE PEOPLE YOU CAN. AS LONG AS EVER YOU CAN."*
>
> *— John Wesley*

CHAPTER 2

The Desired Destiny

FEW OF US, as we travel through life, think of our destiny as the achievement of our life's efforts. Destiny is more than a destination, it is the fulfillment of the purpose for which we have lived. Our "desires" play a major role in our journey through life, and the means by which we exercise our talents and abilities. In many respects, we visualize our destiny through our aspirations and how they are implemented. We are motivated by feelings and inspired by aspirations. One of the great truths that governs our life was revealed by Jesus Christ when He said, "As a man thinks in his heart, so is he."

Each day we take steps that lead us to our future. Whatever we do and how well we do it will define the journey we travel:

- *Are we organized or disorganized?*
- *Are we specifically focused or uncertain of our intentions?*
- *Are we committed to our objectives?*
- *Do we believe in the value of our efforts?*

To be successful, we must believe in the value of our efforts and the specific purposes for which we work. Like many others, I believe we were created for a specific purpose and given the talents and abilities needed to achieve the purpose we were created to fulfill. I believe that God creates each of us for a specific purpose, because we were created in His image and likeness.

Too small a percentage of our population truly perceive this concept, or the possibilities their life contains. We each know individuals who possess a vision of their capacities and, as a result, achieve far more than others believe possible. One very famous and extremely successful man said, laughingly:

"AFTER ONLY THIRTY YEARS OF HARD WORK, I BECAME AN OVERNIGHT SUCCESS."

Each of us is destined for the success we are willing to work to achieve. No one comes into this world as a ready-made failure. We reflect our Creator and our potential is greater than we can imagine. Some seem to know their destiny early in their life. A five-year-old girl was asked what she would be when she grew up. She answered, "I am an artist." An eight-year-old boy explained he was taking piano lessons because he would become a surgeon someday and needed good hands and fingers to perform operations. By far most of us, however, spend time searching for a job that offers an income, and we follow that job until something better arrives. I knew a banker who retired after 40 years and told me he had never enjoyed a year of his profession. He lived in a large house with servants, but was unhappy with his work until the day he retired. So many work for a living without enjoying the work they are doing.

Some years ago I wrote a book titled, *There's More to Life Than Making a Living*. The organization to which I devoted much of my working life purchased many thousands of copies for its employees and Board members within the United States and around the world. It was the purpose of my life to share the value of committed human service as a means of inspiring others to live beyond themselves.

As I counsel and mentor countless individuals in personal and business matters, I often see that many by middle age, or even later, feel they have reached the end of their possibilities. The word "destiny" is never mentioned, yet they often ask how can they redeem their personal, financial, or business life, and how can they overcome their debts, discouragements, and their overwhelming sense of failure. My answer has been: each of us must sincerely and earnestly seek to find our life's purpose. That knowledge, combined with a list of positive traits, talents, and experiences, will open a new concept to a life of success, substance, and significance—a life of greater meaning with greater aspirations. As author George Elliott wrote:

"IT IS NEVER TOO LATE TO BECOME WHAT WE SHOULD HAVE BEEN."

With all personal assessments aside, it is how well we do each day's work that matters the most. If we do each job well, we will increase our ability, build better habits, and strengthen our self-confidence. During the 1940s, the late Dr. Norman Vincent Peale wrote *The Power of Positive Thinking*, a book so controversial that many theologians condemned it, but Dr. Peale's readership grew and his message about living up to the best within us captured the imagination of millions of motivated individuals. I know of one CEO who ordered 500 copies of this book to inspire his employees. I read it several times myself.

During the 1950s, Dr. Maxwell Maltz, a New York City plastic surgeon, noticed that even following surgery to correct an obvious disfigurement, some patients remained convinced that they were still ugly. In his book, *Psychocybernetics*, Dr. Maltz explained that one's thinking and perceptions guide their life and it takes 21 days to reshape or change a thought or habit. This book became an instant bestseller, as the doctor's ideas were adopted by hopeful readers. Today's neuroscientists, who can visualize the brain's physical workings, and various chemical and electrical events that determine its success, affirm that 21 days of new thinking or acting can create a valuable new habit.

In seeking to place more value in each day, the thinking person activates repeated smaller successes, which will equip him for bigger decisions that produce ever-increasing, positive results. Those who do their best to meet each day's challenges will enjoy life more as it progresses. A day that is helter-skelter with poorly performed tasks and unmet obligations, produces a toxic effect on the physical brain, scientists report. The mental and emotional effects of a good day's work cannot be exaggerated. A pattern of such successes leads to a strong, disciplined, well-rounded personality.

Many of us minimize our deficient performances with the excuse that someone else can handle certain tasks better than we can. In this way we diminish our potential. Many successful people believe we should attempt to learn more and do more each year. This is very good for our brain, as it continues to grow and develop as long as we live. Far too many people, however, decrease their habits and activities rather than increasing potential by creative thinking and innovative efforts. Our Creator made no small or unimportant lives. How well the life we live matches the life we envision remains a product of our choices. Each person's destiny is largely created by themselves. Always remember that we create the person we become.

Even those who do not believe in God's guidance and direction have a profound sense of destiny. Certain individuals like Steve Jobs have no particular religious background, yet they sense the seeds of greatness in their lives. At the time the Apple Corporation cofounder was in college, he found himself directionless. The restless young man travelled to India looking for spiritual enlightenment.

He also embarked on various educational searches, seeking to find the road on which his life should travel.

At one point he became interested in calligraphy, the art of producing beautiful handwriting with a pen or brush, which led to his interest in typography and the study of various fonts. For a fertile mind like Jobs, the next step became that of creating something a giant step beyond early computers. The Apple Computer's user could, with a few keystrokes, create graphics as well as typography.

The corporation enjoyed one success after another under Steve Jobs' leadership. However, the Apple Corporation board eventually voted to demote their CEO and he resigned in 1985. Still intent on pursuing his fascination with electronic communication and venturing ever further into entertainment and similar products, Jobs' personal research led him to create a new company called NeXT. This venture succeeded beyond anything he could have imagined. The Apple Corporation was forced to reinstall Jobs as CEO, or allow a competitor to acquire an enormous leap forward. The creative genius within a man like Steve Jobs impels him toward seeking, exploring, and discovering his unique destiny, one which in this case has affected every person alive.

As we work at our assigned tasks each day, we might have little idea that such mundane work has anything to do with a great destiny or even an interesting life. From age 12 onward, as I grew toward manhood on that isolated Minnesota farm, I was needed to perform hard labor seven days a week. Cutting and stacking firewood, hauling water from the pump house to our home, studying by lamplight, cultivating fields and harvesting crops, feeding hogs, birthing calves, and milking cows twice each day seemed to offer no hope for a desirable future, much less a desired destiny.

At age 14, I questioned my mother as to what this endless drudgery meant for my life. She advised me to ask God what His purpose for me would be. I prayed this prayer: "Dear Father, help me find the purpose for my life." At the age of 18, I began to pray, "Dear Father, help me do the best I can, with what I have, where I am, at all times." I would attempt to do my best with what I had but I could not visualize what my life could be beyond the front gate of our farm.

As I recounted in my book, *Hope, Desire, and Aspire*, eventually it became amazingly apparent to me that everything I experienced during the dozen years of my lost boyhood would become the foundation for an exceedingly blessed, prosperous, and significant life and career. I now see that every ounce of hard labor, self-discipline, competition, and eagerness to learn were to come into play as I walked toward my own unique destiny. It took decades to recognize that my simple prayers were being answered throughout my working life. So it is in countless other lives as we answer our own prayers in the process of living. Whatever we do with what we have is preparing us for a larger, more prosperous life.

We build our future one day at a time by the thoughts we think, the decisions we make, the words we speak, and every task we perform. For each of us, as we travel toward our destination, anything we envision, anything we pursue with dedicated efforts and determined faith, is possible. As Christ told us, what we believe is what we become. If a farm boy with little education, studying his lessons by lamplight, and praying for help in finding his purpose, could one day help millions have a better life—you can do whatever you believe you can do.

Your destiny, as my destiny, is largely in our hands, in our hearts, and in our minds. We were each created to fulfill a specific purpose, and we were given the needed talents and abilities to do so. If you will believe in yourself and in the value of your life, your destiny will prove worthy of your finest efforts. As you ask for guidance, be thankful for the guidance you've received. As you begin each day, give thanks for the opportunities that are before you. As you do whatever you do, give thanks for the ability to do it. Your life is your greatest blessing—use it to the best of your ability in every way you can.

"IT'S NOT WHAT YOU KNOW BUT THE KIND OF JOB YOU DO THAT MAKES THE DIFFERENCE."

— Dr. Ben Carson

CHAPTER 3

The Power of Your Mind

YOU CAN DO almost anything you desire to do. Each of us came into the world with a mind equipped to think, to learn, to decide, and to accomplish anything within reason. The miracle of our mind is the source of our consciousness: every impression, every view and vision, every creative concept, idea, opinion, evaluation, hope, or aspiration is contained in the thoughts that reside in our mind. Each person's mind is structured to their own reality. The amazing difference in human personalities reflects the endless diversities of our individual minds. Your mind contains the thoughts that control your life. You increase the capacity of your mind through your education, training, experience, and the wise investment of your thoughts in subjects that inspire your imagination and focus your attention on your talents and the abilities you possess.

Small children use their minds almost without stopping. They soak up knowledge like sponges. They imagine, explore, take risks, and are willing to fall endless times before they learn to walk, climb, or ride a bike. Somewhere along the way, many of us lose most of these traits because of adult influences, authority figures, and dozens of other reasons that relate to other peoples' influence. The fact is that few among us realize the importance of having a well-trained, disciplined, and continually developing mind.

The late Dr. Karl Menninger, founder of the world-famous Menninger Clinic in Topeka, Kansas, pioneered in bringing mental health issues to public attention. His newspaper columns taught readers how to protect and nourish their minds. He often advocated taking an annual review of one's life, listing personal successes, dissatisfactions, and areas that needed improvement. These simple, commonsense ideas might have seemed too simplistic to bother with at a time when mentally ill patients were routinely sent to mental institutions or given shock treatments. As Dr. Menninger said:

> *"MOST OF MY LIFE HAS BEEN SPENT IN TREATING PERSONS ONE BY ONE. BUT AS I BECOME INCREASINGLY AWARE OF THE EXTENT OF MISERY AND HOPELESSNESS IN OUR SOCIETY, I THINK MORE OF PREVENTING UNNECESSARY SUFFERING AT THE SOURCE, BEFORE INDIVIDUALS TAKE OR ARE FORCED TO TAKE THE WRONG ROAD."*

Today, with mental health advancements widely known and practiced, Dr. Menninger's yearly overview idea seems completely reasonable. Ask anyone about areas of personal life that need improvement and most have a ready answer:

- *Finances*
- *Time*
- *Overwork*
- *Unpleasant relationships*
- *Failing marriages*
- *Unruly children*

The mind is the only instrument supplied to each of us which can understand and solve the most complicated and delicate of all human problems. Keeping one's mind active, fit, and resourceful should be a consistent goal for everyone, yet many of us never think about it. We must learn to equip ourselves to overcome obstacles, solve problems, set goals, and achieve objectives. It is our choice, yours and mine, to do what we can and do it to the best of our ability.

Each person comes into the world with extraordinary mental potential. It is how we use our mind that determines the outcome of our life. Even those with brain damage at birth, or those whose brain has been damaged by alcohol, pain killers, prescription or street drugs, can be improved or even healed. The good news is, as our mind's capacities increase, our success, substance, and lifetime significance continues to increase in relation to our efforts and commitment. The things we do today that have favorable outcomes will influence our mind's capacity tomorrow. Years ago, Émile Coué, a French psychologist with a popular following, urged people to say continually:

"EVERY DAY, IN EVERY WAY, I'M GETTING BETTER AND BETTER."

That is a good practice as far as it goes. If every day in every way you do what you do better, more mindfully, more completely, more satisfactorily, you will improve your life immeasurably. One of the basic points in Dr. Menninger's approach to mental and emotional illness was the role of parents:

"IT IS MUCH EASIER, MORE LOGICAL, AND MORE EFFICACIOUS TO HELP A CHILD GROW UP WITH LOVE AND COURAGE THAN IT IS TO INSTILL HOPE IN A DESPONDENT SOUL. WHAT MOTHER AND FATHER MEAN TO THEM IS MORE THAN PSYCHIATRISTS CAN EVER MEAN."

It is important for us to understand that the youthful mind is the most receptive mind. The average person gains 50 percent of his adult intelligence before the age of 15. The good news is that the sooner you begin to improve your mind with the thoughts you place there, the more successful and productive you will become. The longer you delay this positive procedure, the less effective it will be. There are some things we lose in the aging process, as well as some things we gain. We should never waste time when our mind and thoughts are concerned. The mental habits we form become the most influential and controlling aspects of our life.

We can learn anything we desire to learn. We can change toxic mental habits, depression which leads to inertia, and negative thinking which persuades a person that it is impossible to accomplish what is possible to accomplish. Such unrealistic thoughts are diminishing and destructive.

An Illinois businessman, successful in a highly responsible profession, could hardly bring himself to speak to others. He was a second-generation American of German descent, but spoke English with a pronounced accent. His self-consciousness concerning that accent led him to believe that no one, especially not a woman, could be interested in such a backward personality. He seldom dated, but eventually found himself interested in a woman who told him that she loved his deep voice and charming accent. They got married and the man's personality changed almost immediately. His wife liked him to read aloud to her and he quickly learned the pleasure of conversation. This carried over into office friendships. Eventually he could joke with others as he told stories in his highly exaggerated accent. He did not change at all, but when his mind changed, his perceptions of himself changed, and his life dramatically changed.

Changes in personal mindsets affect not only the individual but families, business associates, and communities, and ripples far beyond our imagination. A self-employed father of four found himself working 60 to 80 hours a week to support the growing needs of his children ages 4 to 12. He and his wife agreed early in their marriage that she would be a full-time wife and mother. Pressures mounted as the man faced such realities as the rising cost of everything from hot dogs to ballet shoes, athletic gear to tuitions.

When his oldest daughter had behavior problems at school, he found himself at a loss, as she said, "What do you care, Dad? You're not here anyway." This family crisis had to be solved. There seemed to be no way this father could find extra time for anything and his workload was essential to keeping the family ship afloat. After his anger and dismay subsided, he called a family meeting and allowed each child to express their needs for more of his time. The family calendar showed his wife on perpetual carpool duty, zigzagging among tight schedules and endless after-school requirements. Both parents felt exhausted.

As they talked, the father realized he had to lead in creating family time when it seemed each day's calendar was full for each family member. He decreed that the first Saturday of each month would be set aside for family activities. A soccer game or ballet recital would require all to attend, otherwise the family would decide together on the day's activities. Everyone would participate and none would object or quarrel. They called those activities exploring and each voted on where they would go. They saw a horse farm and riding academy; they toured the state capital; visited museums; listened to street music; and tiptoed into quiet, old church sanctuaries to view beautiful, stained-glass windows and ancient furnishings. They spent little money but walked enough miles to bring everyone home tired but refreshed.

The father's summation: "In four months I lost four days' work but gained priceless knowledge about my children. The youngest is loud and aggressive and I assumed he was highly competitive until the day he refused to play a game. He said, 'I like to win, and my brother and sisters always beat me at everything.' I heard the other children inspire and challenge their little brother. I learned that two of my children love art and the oldest invited me to read some things she had written."

The reward for working through a problem by using a good mind and the desire to do the best a father and mother could do for their family began to bind them together in new and creative ways. The children drew closer to one another, and the parents observed their beautiful offspring with gratitude and pride. The father's picture of his family changed from problematic, costly, and chaotic, to one of relaxed and confident well-being for all six members.

The act of problem solving with unilateral or communal decisions occurs virtually every day of our lives. Decisions not made, actions not taken, or refusal to involve oneself with others, decreases our brain power and weakens our overall effectiveness. Doing our best, even if we fail, increases our mental effectiveness. Life is on-the-job training. Promotion comes when we learn to do the best we can with what we have.

Problem solving can begin as young as kindergarten. A four-year-old boy, happy about an upcoming automobile trip, wanted to take all his toys to grandmother's house. His father averted an expected tantrum by handing the child a wooden box in which he could carry his toys in the car. For days the boy happily put as many of his toys as he could into the box, trying one group after another. When he unpacked his treasures upon arrival, no one could understand how anyone could load that many objects into a small space without an engineering degree!

If small children can be challenged to use their minds in creative ways, adults should be willing to expand their mental capacities and progress in their efforts to achieve their major objectives. If each of us will attempt to solve a negative habit or ongoing problem each month, we will improve ourselves far beyond our limited expectations.

As we increase our mental activities, we increase our life's perspective and the range of our mind's activities. We learn to do more things better, more efficiently, more pleasantly, and more enjoyably. By doing our best with what we have, we extend our life outward and increase our capacity to encourage and support others in positive and productive ways. This teaches us to desire the best from ourselves, for our family, our friends, and others. This increases our faith in ourselves as we enable others to see and expect miracles within their own lives. It is by stepping forward, doing our best, and believing in ourselves and others that we meet with unexpected blessings. Too many people talk the talk but fail to walk the walk. Our mind creates a chain of life events as we believe and speak the noble thoughts we think. If we do not do what we say, however, the chain of our intentions becomes broken and useless. What we do each day matters tremendously. Each undone task, unspoken word of encouragement, or neglected decision depletes our mental intentions and our day's effectiveness. Let your mind and noble thoughts instruct you on how to do all things well. We owe that much to ourselves and to the world in which we live.

> *"BELIEVE IT CAN BE DONE. WHEN YOU BELIEVE SOMETHING CAN BE DONE, REALLY BELIEVE. YOUR MIND WILL FIND THE WAYS TO DO IT. BELIEVING A SOLUTION PAVES THE WAY TO A SOLUTION."*
>
> *— DAVID J. SCHWARTZ*
> *THE MAGIC OF THINKING BIG*

CHAPTER 4

Dreams and Visions

IF A FOUR-YEAR-OLD boy can decide how to pack his travel box and fit everything in, this proves it is never too early or too late to visualize our next achievement or our life's destiny. The earlier we learn to dream dreams and see visions, the better it is for us. The sooner we begin visualizing worthy objectives or greater aspirations, the richer and fuller our lives become.

A farmer will visualize his future crops and increased herds of livestock: so many calves and colts, so many fields and acres of corn, oats, and wheat. These predictable visions operate against a backdrop of the unpredictable: late snows, tornadoes, early frost, and dry weather—all factors of nature over which he has no control. Nevertheless, each season proves there can be no growth, no increase, and no prosperity without visualizing a beneficial outcome.

Such early lessons, in large part, prepared me for my own destiny—that of guiding thousands of America's business leaders and other professionals in funding multimillion-dollar community projects. I began this career in my late 20s and found myself advising men and women far more accomplished and experienced than I was. To my great astonishment, I saw that many community goals had seldom been reached, nor did anyone ever expect to oversubscribe a substantial financial objective. At first it was difficult for me to understand why goals would be established with little hope of being reached.

As I struggled to discover why such successful people in their own professions did not expect that a worthwhile community goal could be reached, I soon saw the obvious reasons for failure. Each knew what they could envision for their own companies, yet had no ability to project their vision beyond the realm of their own endeavors. In thinking about raising funds for multimillion-dollar projects, their vision focused primarily on the financial aspect of the project, and their doubts focused on the support of the business and professional members of their communities. Someone had to help them visualize and realize the potential value of the facilities to be constructed, and the way they would benefit those whom they would serve. They had to be convinced of the intrinsic importance of the project to be undertaken, and in their ability to persuade others to help make it possible. Once they enthusiastically embraced what they saw in their minds, the rest was to follow. Invariably, once the leadership embraced and visualized the completion of their important objective, instead of focusing on the needed finances, in every instance successful completion was achieved.

For over 40 years I listened to and learned from some of the most brilliant entrepreneurial leaders in America, yet often I found that I was dealing with those who doubted when it came to significant community outreach. This was understandable, since individuals of that caliber do not buy "a pig in a poke." Only through visualizing something they never had thought about, and only through imagining the good it would do, would such individuals venture into uncharted waters with uncertain outcomes. Throughout my career, I sought the support of great minds and great hearts willing to imagine the wonderful things they could accomplish for the benefit of their communities, and those who would benefit from their generous efforts. As the great missionary William A. Carey once said:

"EXPECT GREAT THINGS FROM GOD; ATTEMPT GREAT THINGS FOR GOD."

Much later in my experience I encountered one of the most difficult and challenging situations I had ever faced. This problem created tremendous dissension among the business and civic leaders of the Tidewater Area. The city of Norfolk, Virginia, had condemned The Salvation Army's property for a major Urban Renewal Project. This meant The Salvation Army would need to conduct a fundraising effort to build a new Headquarters and Community Service Center. I had been engaged to raise the required funds.

For several years the United Way had intended to conduct a major capital campaign for all the United Way agencies needing to expand their facilities. However, they were unable to find the right person willing to serve as Chairman of such a large, consolidated community effort. They had forbidden any of the United Way agencies to conduct their own Capital Campaign or expand their facilities. We were denied the ability to conduct our campaign because the United Way had indicated it would conduct a single, combined campaign for all the United Way agencies. Because of this commitment, the United Way forbade The Salvation Army to undertake the campaign I was engaged to conduct.

One of the members of The Salvation Army's Advisory Board was also a member of the United Way's Board of Directors. The more I realized how much the community would suffer, and saw the hard feelings that were developing, the more I sought a workable solution. I met with the man who served on both Boards and proposed to him that I conduct the combined campaign that the United Way had proposed, at no additional cost, as a good will offering for their support and cooperation.

His response was: "Do you think such an offer is possible and do you think the United Way Board of Directors will accept your offer?" My response was that he present my offer to the Chairman of the United Way's Board and allow me to speak to their entire

Board of Directors. A special meeting was called and I spoke to the Board and offered my services at no additional cost to them. In closing, I handed the chairman a list of ten men who had served as chairmen of campaigns I had recently conducted, and asked that he contact each before a decision was made.

Within a week I received a call from the Chairman of the United Way Board, asking if I would meet with him and explain exactly how the combined campaign would be conducted. He told me of the man they had sought to be the Chairman of the Combined Capital Campaign and how he had continually refused. I knew of the man because he was the same person I wanted to serve as the Chairman of The Salvation Army's Capital Campaign.

God works in mysterious ways. The wife of the man I hoped would become chairman of my Salvation Army Campaign was the President of one of the agencies that would be included in the Combined Capital Campaign. Shortly after the Combined Campaign was announced, she asked if she could meet with me concerning her involvement. When I told her I wanted her husband as the chairman, she explained why he had previously refused. I asked who his closest friends were. I discovered his banker had served as my chairman in Charlottesville, Virginia, and his most respected friend was the former Governor of Virginia and had served as the President of the University of Virginia. I asked her to pray with me and ask for divine guidance. I contacted each of these men and together they helped me enlist Frank Batten, Chairman of Landmark Communications and founder of the Weather Channel, to become the chairman of the most successful Capital Campaign ever conducted in Norfolk, Virginia.

I learned much about the power of our mind's imagination and its capacity to visualize and conceptualize. The landmarks within the communities in which I conducted Capital Campaigns stand out in my mind as I see the tangible benefits hundreds of thousands of individuals have received from the various institutions we have created and expanded. These benefits originated in peoples' hearts, minds, ideas, dreams, and visions. Human efforts, hard work, occasional disagreements, and often forbidding economic conditions, never inhibited any of the projects I undertook during the 40 years of my professional life. They were all built and exist today because of the force of human visualization and the efforts of generous and talented individuals who believed in their cities and communities. None of our campaigns ever failed. With God's help, the average campaign reached 169 percent of its stated objective.

Dreams too large for most people to handle come and go during most peoples' lives. A dream arrives, a great idea emerges most unexpectedly, and gets shoved aside unexamined. The recipient immediately believes that their idea is impossible: too big, too costly, too laborious, too few people to agree with it. Millions of dreams die stillborn, but the relatively few that grow into reality change the world. They come about through the process of visualization: step by step, often over the course of years, as the creator encounters problems, hardship, disbelief, scorn, and every form of discouragement. The individual willing to persevere despite every setback, meanwhile, learns to overcome anything and everything that stands in their way. As Thomas Edison said to one scoffer, who alluded to his numerous failed experiments:

"AT LEAST I KNOW 99 THINGS THAT DON'T WORK."

Visionary people seek the fulfillment of their vision without expecting public applause or admiration as it goes forward. Such great people understand that ordinary consensus is important for most, but for the visionary mind to continually expand it must seek the company of other forward thinkers. As an old proverb states:

"WATER SEEKS ITS OWN LEVEL."

Doing all we can with our mind means taking note of lessons learned from people of achievement, from inspiring books, past experience, and the wisdom gained from problem solving. Each of us has opportunities to solve problems, both large and small, each day. Ask a young child how to solve some unique dilemma and you might get an applicable solution. A child is curious, observant, and wonders how things work. A child has not been trained to think as others have been trained to think. Parents who teach their children how to solve their own problems often learn a lot from their offspring's thoughts. Young minds and fresh ideas are often amazingly creative and practical.

Susan Speros, one of four children of a Greek-American father, recalls him as a man of high energy and entrepreneurial instincts, always looking for a new business venture, invention, or a way to make money for the family. Her father supported his family with one small business after another, and instilled a family habit Susan well remembers.

"We would sit around the family table, the six of us, as Dad talked about a new idea or business; together we would try and name the new business. All of us, including my Mom, offered ideas and ways to improve on my father's ideas. These were great times and wonderful memories. It was fun and we were all glad to be involved in the discussions for his new business venture. Dad was very creative and savvy at marketing. He would lead us, encourage us to think, and often chuckle with excitement over launching something new. Maybe it's not surprising that his three daughters and son all grew up to have their own successful businesses."

Susan's entrepreneurial instincts came into full force when she moved to Savannah, Georgia, to be the manager of a telecommunications company. This job soon ended because the Atlanta-based headquarters went out of business. Quickly, she was approached about starting and managing a new Savannah telephone company. She had already been working in the industry for several years and knew the ins and outs of the business very well, so she had no hesitation. She named the business, hired the technicians, sold the systems, oversaw the installations, and built quite a following. The new business was growing; however, she was not the owner. The owner was not making good on promises he had made in the beginning, so she left.

In 1984, in the sunroom of her Ardsley park house, and armed only with her spirit for entrepreneurial endeavors, her abilities and passion for the telecom industry, and her desire to win and succeed, she started the Speros Company. With very little money, but a ton of knowledge on how the relatively new telecom business operated, she began consulting with large Savannah firms. Educating them on the ins and outs of billing, tariffs, features, ways, and cost, they found they could save money on their skyrocketing monthly phone bills. One client at a time, one new employee at a time, she marketed, consulted, and built a reputation for her company because she knew the telephone business and was eager to serve other business owners.

Throughout the next several years, new technology services were added as the need arose. Susan's ability to embrace the change in the industry has led them into not only business telephone system sales, but IT servers, support and sales, surveillance camera systems, website design, carrier sales, and their latest offering with AV.

The name Speros has become synonymous for technology in Savannah. Just like her father before her, she is still forward thinking and always looking for new business opportunities. Her parents would be proud. She continues to succeed, and now employs over 30 people and grosses close to $5 million in sales a year.

Million dollar ideas, opportunities, and ventures are within almost anyone's grasp. School children start thriving businesses on their computers these days. Older people who worked for years at ordinary projects suddenly burst forth with something other people want or need and find themselves immediately successful. As Henry J. Kaiser said:

"FIND A NEED AND FILL IT."

Those of us who start out as I did, apprehensive about a lack of education and experience, must learn quickly how to overcome these real or perceived deficits. My method was to ask a leading question of the older and impressively successful person who sat before me. As he expounded, I listened carefully and learned, not only about our mutual project, but about the man and his thinking. This became a continuing education for me as I worked and grew into my role of advising people I greatly admired on how to fulfill community visions. In the beginning, I was so much aware of my own deficiencies that I asked a kindly librarian to recommend books from which I could learn more about business, management, personal relationships, and visionary objectives. Her advice helped so much that I have enjoyed keeping up with business in its many forms throughout the years. She helped me understand that education is a lifetime learning experience.

Mention any subject about which you know or are curious, think of any interesting person you should know more about or business you should study, and today you will find endless streams of new information and a wealth of new books, as well as old classics, online. Anyone, anywhere can strengthen their mind and imagination, and obtain new ideas for making their unseen visions into realities.

In rare instances a person will report being awakened in the middle of the night with a new idea or solution to an apparently impossible problem. During a regional recession several years ago, a commercial real estate agent found himself unable to buy or sell property, since the banks were not lending money. As months passed, despite all his best efforts, his family needed such necessities as tuition, shoes, and automobile repairs. His wife began to sell their inherited antiques. The family looked shabby and the man felt increasingly desperate.

One night he prayed for an answer to his problems. He went to bed and at 3:00 a.m. awoke from a sound sleep for no apparent reason. Wide awake, he seemed to receive an instruction that he should fly to New York and obtain a $2.8 million loan to buy a large property for his client. He slid out of bed and quietly began to dress. His wife stirred in her sleep and he told her he was going to New York and would return that evening. He drove to the airport, wondering if his credit card would be accepted, or if he was foolish to make the trip. Miraculously, he bought a ticket and arrived in Manhattan just as the city began to awaken. He bought a cup of coffee and a bagel, enjoyed them slowly, then walked down Fifth Avenue to one of the city's major banks. Just as he approached the door, it opened and a gentleman asked, "How can I help you?"

"I need a loan officer," he replied.

"That would be me," the gentleman answered.

Less than 30 minutes later, the loan applicant left the bank and returned home, able to consummate his first business deal in many months. He believed this event to be an astonishing answer to prayer.

Daphene Jones also awoke for no reason at 3:00 a.m. one memorable day. At the time she held a medium-level corporate job, for which she won awards, but had no idea about advancing to even mid-level management.

"I came wide awake for no reason with a tremendous idea in my head. The idea could not have come out of me. I don't know how to think that way. I felt so amazed and awed that I got out of bed to find a pen and paper. I wrote down my thoughts in detail, because I was afraid I would fall asleep and forget all of it. Also, I was curious to re-read what I had written, because I had a lifelong belief that I was sort of cute but dumb. It was amazing to me that I could hold down a job and even get an award."

Daphene's dream dazzled her, but also impressed her. She showed what she had written to a businessman friend and he said it looked impressive. She needed a business plan, he told her, and she asked what that might be. At that point, Daphene, little educated and battling severe problems with low self-esteem, easily might have abandoned her vision. Instead she learned how to write a compelling business plan. "I didn't know how to write a business letter, much less a business plan."

DJ Consultants, Inc. officially became a business on January 1, 1992. To make it easier for people to remember her name, she decided to change her name for business to DJ instead of Daphene. God had given her a unique ability to simplify how companies managed time and information.

Weeks later, by divine accident, she related part of her vision to an exercise buddy. The woman held a corporate position that opened the door for Daphene's first presentation. She immediately had to learn how to present her idea before a board, even how to dress for business success. It all came too fast for most people to assimilate, but Daphene doggedly persisted.

Her first presentation earned her a major corporate contract, not only in headquarters but other major cities throughout the United States. Daphene, admittedly intimidated, took a deep breath and resigned her job. She plunged into her new venture full of trepidation, hope, and amazement at how well she could put over her ideas. One recommendation followed another and several years later she ended up living on the Upper East Side in

Manhattan. By now she had two large corporations for clients and had hired several employees. Traveling all the time was difficult. She laughed, since she had grown up in West Texas and was now living in the "Big Apple."

Daphene's dream did not lead her into taking small steps toward completing her vision. It took several giant steps, it seemed to her, to bring her vision into reality. In recent years, Daphene Jones has spoken to audiences across America, made numerous television appearances, and written a book. She believed God used the vision He poured into her to make her able to grow into the woman she is today. She humbly believes that whereas all things are possible with God, the impossible can only be overcome if one is willing to seek spiritual guidance.

"That dream not only changed my ordinary life circumstances but, most importantly, it changed me. This has blessed every member of my family, the people I work with, and my story has inspired many of the thousands in my various audiences. I hate to think how different it would be if I had just gone back to sleep. It is hard to comprehend that as of January 1, 2017, DJ Consultants, Inc. is celebrating 25 years. After being told by many people that 'start-up' companies seldom make it, I am thankful I listened to God, who became the CEO."

I wonder how many of us pray for dreams and visions. Some few, just before sleeping, ask for a good dream. Others find they often receive good ideas or solutions to problems as they sleep or while taking a shower or driving a car. Some keep pen and paper handy to record such illusive ideas, or speak them into a recording device. People who seek solutions and ideas surely find them. People who wait for them to arrive seldom find much.

If you want bigger more productive dreams, ask. If you need creative solutions, direct your mind to seek them. If you desire advanced and more creative thinking, surround yourself with such thinkers. Knock on the doors of those who inspire you. Almost invariably, the doors open to ever-widening vistas.

Three of America's most creative thinkers understood this truth. Thomas Edison, Harvey Firestone, and Henry Ford built adjoining vacation houses in the small Florida town of Fort Myers. The three giants of invention enjoyed spending hours of recreation, friendship, and good conversation each winter for many years. If you desire bigger dreams and more fulfillment, do likewise. Move out of the ordinary and into the widest place your mind can imagine. You and your imagination are built to achieve literally anything. Lift your own limits and aspirations.

> **"WHATEVER THE MIND CAN CONCEIVE AND BELIEVE, IT CAN ACHIEVE."**
>
> *— Napoleon Hill*

CHAPTER 5

Body and Soul

MENS SANA IN corpore sano. This well-known Latin motto, means "a sound mind in a sound body." Our mind directs the way we treat or mistreat our body. Fortunately, recent decades have convinced most of us that a holistic attitude is essential. Science continues to offer more and more absolute proof that the ancient Greeks, who believed and celebrated the idea that our minds are limitless and our bodies should reflect equal value, are still admired today. Countless millions worldwide eagerly follow the Olympic Games, which for centuries have challenged individuals to stretch their capacities and attempt to shatter past records.

We may not be an Einstein or an Olympic athlete, but the ancient Greeks were correct. At any stage of life we can challenge our minds and bodies to respond to our desired outcomes. A 90-year-old woman suffered a mild stroke and sat despondent and unwilling to speak or help herself. Her daughters could not persuade her to respond to their loving attentions.

One day one of her girls fastened one-pound weights around her mother's wrists and said, "You may be in a wheelchair today, but you are very strong and need to exercise a little to help you get back to where you were." She showed her mother how to do simple arm lifts, five at a time. "This strengthens your heart," she told her. When she returned two days later, she found her mother was a changed woman. She was relaxed, proud of herself, and boasted that she could do ten reps each time.

"Your muscles don't know how old they are," her daughter assured her. "You are making a comeback."

Our purpose here is not to persuade the reader of the value of nutrition, exercise, and sleep, which most mothers teach us very early; rather it is to remind us that wherever any of us are at any time, our mind has already nagged us to do whatever it is we've been postponing. Some of the smallest changes reap the biggest mind-body rewards. For example, adding one hours' sleep to a nightly regime increases mental acuity and job performance to a remarkable degree. Continuing to postpone an exercise plan can result in such undesirable states as high blood pressure or Type 2 diabetes. These ideas are not news, but too many of us ignore facts.

The news today is that the brain is fueled by whatever we choose to eat. "You are what you eat" has been said for years, but now science has proved a direct connection between nutrition and brain power. The human soul is defined as "mind, will, and emotions," all of which determine the future of our present-day physical self. In the south where I now live, soul food denotes good eating, meaning black-eyed peas, turnip greens, cornbread, and whatever else delights the appetite and emotions. More realistically, our soul food should include the best thoughts our minds can conceive, a will strong enough to pursue our best efforts, and emotions that allow us to enjoy simple pleasures: the pleasure of the best and healthiest foods we can find and work and play that increases our physical strength and produces satisfaction and joy.

Many of us come to a rude awakening physically before we allow our minds to take over. One well-known man I know happened to glance in a mirror on the morning of his 40th birthday. He suddenly realized that he looked much older than his years. Jim, as I'll call him, was a hard-driving businessman who promised himself he would become a millionaire by age 30 and had achieved his goal. The following decade saw his successes steadily increasing and his community demands and prestigious opportunities added far more to his overcrowded schedule than he could afford physically or mentally.

But at his office he could not forget the person he saw in his mirror that morning. He tried to believe the strained expression, sagging shoulders, and paunchy stomach simply reflected his late birthday party the night before. Jim could not continue to lie to himself, however. He took stock of his life and realized his successes had brought him to a tipping point. He could change his lifestyle now or suffer the consequences. That day he established a one-year goal. He would be in top shape one year later.

During the intervening year, he had a complete physical workup, hired a personal trainer and nutritionist, set up a basement gym, and relentlessly followed his plan. He saw pounds drop away, his muscles firm up, and he experienced new feelings of energy and well-being. Of course he met his goal, as Jim always did, and by age 41, he looked and felt like a new man. By far his biggest bonus, however, was the fact that he worked out with his 15-year-old son under their trainer's direction. Jim's greatest satisfaction is his memory of that year in which he and his son competed, bonded man-to-man with one another, and rose to a new level of love and respect.

Ask yourself if you've ever been too tired to love. The overfatigued, depressed, or fearful person, the individual harboring anger, resentment, jealousy, or unforgiveness, drives sound health away. It is not always easy to overcome such emotions as these, especially when we are right, but unless we learn to forgive ourselves, each will take their toll on our mental and physical well-being. Toxic emotions attack the body in multiple ways. Such feelings exert chemical and hormonal changes among the cells of our body. This is not theory, it is a medical fact that can readily be shown by today's imaging techniques.

The mind determines far more about our feelings and emotions than most of us realize. It literally determines how our body looks, feels, and performs. It decides what we do each day for better or worse. It tells us to use the stairs to reach our third-floor office. It advises us not to reach for something chocolate or something alcoholic to improve our mood. It instructs us to observe regular sleeping habits and to enjoy maximum physical and mental performance.

A sound mind in a sound body optimizes our optimism. Happiness and well-being spring from good health. Dr. Martin Seligman, in his book *Learned Optimism*, notes that political races, corporate advancements, and high levels of business success are usually obtained by optimists. Whether it's their personal belief system or the effects their personalities have on other people I cannot say, but most of us agree that optimists rule the day.

Negative thinking, especially self-criticism, blame, and condemnation, are proven enemies of our thoughts and emotions. Dr. Caroline Leaf, noted neurocognitive researcher, practitioner, and best-selling author of *Who Switched Off My Brain?* declares the words "I can't" to be the most damaging messages the mind sends to the brain and body. Imagine "I can't" as the moment the conductor halts the engine and all the cars come to a screeching halt. If two small words can stop every function of our life in one moment, imagine the power within the remainder of our verbal instructions to our brain.

Several years ago I learned the amazing power of saying, "I love you" to friends I truly loved and even some acquaintances I admire. All my life I have felt my love and known the strength of my love, but I felt it inappropriate to put it into words that might be misunderstood. But such misunderstanding has never occurred. The people to whom I express my love respond in kind and feelings. The strong current produced by the most powerful words in any language exerts benefits far beyond its expression. "I love you," "I believe in you," "I am proud of you" benefit both the giver and receiver alike. Saying what we honestly feel expands our emotional content tremendously. It releases our finest feelings, even as it vanishes less worthwhile ones. As we grow in love, we grow in optimism and confidence. We see the best in others and learn to find the good in the worst of circumstances.

Admiral Chester Nimitz, was the newly appointed Commander in Chief of the Pacific Fleet when the Japanese bombed Pearl Harbor. On Christmas Day in 1941, Admiral Nimitz was given a boat tour of the destruction. As the tour boat returned, a young helmsman asked, "Well, Admiral, what do you think after seeing all this destruction?"

Nimitz's reply shocked everyone. He said, "The Japanese made three of the biggest mistakes an attack force could ever make, or God was taking care of America. Which do you think it was?"

The young helmsman asked, "What do mean by saying the Japanese made the three biggest mistakes an attack force ever made?"

Nimitz explained, "Mistake number one: the Japanese attacked on Sunday morning. Nine out of every ten crewmen from those ships were ashore on leave. If those same ships had been lured to sea and been sunk, we would have lost 38,000 men instead of 3,800.

"Mistake number two: when the Japanese saw all those battleships lined in a row, they got so carried away sinking those battleships, they never once bombed our dry docks opposite those ships. If they had destroyed our dry docks, we would have had to tow every one of those ships to America to be repaired. As it is now, the ships are in shallow water and can be raised. One tug can pull them over to the dry docks and we can have them repaired and at sea by the time we could have towed them to America. And I already have crews ashore anxious to man those ships.

"Mistake number three: every drop of fuel in the Pacific theater of war is in the ground storage tanks five miles away over that hill. One attack plane could have strafed those tanks and destroyed our fuel supply. That's why I say the Japanese made three of the biggest mistakes an attack force could make or God was taking care of America."

You may have noticed that the optimists you know often are those who give the most. Those who expect great things in their own lives usually give generously to others. The habit of doing all one can for others paves the way to abundance and freedom of spirit that desires more for everyone they meet. Our giving may be tangible or intangible, but it's the timing, the sincerity, and the intuitive understanding that counts the most.

A businesswoman sent a thank-you gift to a high-level official who had helped her. "She sent a beautiful potted plant for my desk. No one else ever gave me something for my office and this plant makes the room come alive," he said. The gift was imaginative and appreciated. Among all the people who sought this man's influence, one person reciprocated in a delightful and meaningful way.

Film actor Sylvester Stallone is another person who demonstrates that passion must be coupled with perseverance for a goal to be reached. He was discouraged and rejected many times, but with great tenacity and determination, success did not elude him for long. Stallone works to create a better world not only through his films, but through the character and attitude he displayed throughout his path to success. He struggled especially when first starting out as an actor and screenwriter, as many do, but his attitude of never giving up—which Stallone represents on and off the screen—has always been at the core of his success.

His support of various charitable events and foundations is well-known. At one event held for the Canadian Diabetes Association in February 2012, he managed to raise a total of $100,000! He is also a big supporter of the Pediatric Epilepsy Project, a foundation that helps children with epilepsy to battle and cope with the disorder and conducts research to better understand the condition. It has been said that Stallone makes a habit of doing at least one kindness a day. Such consistent decisions amount to real soul food: ways to feed his mind, his will, and his emotions.

As we expand our human souls, our body responds to healthy thinking and emotional joy. Giving anything to anyone, even a sincere "I love you," relaxes muscles with endorphins. It has been said that each of us needs 15 hugs each day for maximum mental health. In our fast-paced world, few people receive the hugs they need. However, there are other ways to receive that love. America has the world's largest dog and cat populations. Emotions between pet owners and their adopted canines and felines cannot be adequately described or explained. The fact is love and attention between humans and animals invariably expand the lives of each. As Dave Barry wrote:

"YOU CAN SAY ANY FOOLISH THING TO A DOG, AND THE DOG WILL GIVE YOU A LOOK THAT SAYS, 'WOW, YOU'RE RIGHT! I NEVER WOULD'VE THOUGHT OF THAT!'"

Obviously, while walking or lifting weights, both excellent for the body, few of us bother to think about our souls. Indisputably, however, the balance among mind, will, and emotions is a delicate one, subject to moment-by-moment change. The onset of a cold leaves most of us feeling intellectually and emotionally irritable and flat. Just as low health affects the mind, our minds greatly affect our overall health. Soul food is none too plentiful in an over-stressed person who lives in a body that is under par. Which part of your soul predominates? We all know the intellectual who seldom seems to offer any emotion, the strong-willed individual who acts first and thinks later, or the person who seems to be led around by the nose through his or her strong emotions.

Overbalance in any one of the soul's three areas affects us physically. Observe the teenager who becomes lovesick. He or she seems not to think about anything, seems unwilling to initiate much activity, and emotionally seems to live on a distant planet. The term "lovesick" might not exist in a medical dictionary, but obviously affects every aspect of the sufferer's life.

Healthy love, by contrast, offers new energy, ebullience, joy, happiness, and a pervasive sense of well-being. Love can be recommended as the best antidote to life's many trials and tribulations. Doing all we can in a positive manner invariably offers countless ways to express simple acts of love. In fact, it can turn enemies into friends. How can asking for a favor change a negative attitude into a positive attitude? How can requesting kindness cause a person to change his or her opinion of you? The answer to what generates The Benjamin Franklin Effect is the answer to much more than why you do what you do. As Benjamin Franklin proposed:

"THE BEST WAY TO TURN AN ENEMY INTO A FRIEND IS TO ASK HIM TO DO YOU A FAVOR."

Most of us know what best feeds our souls. Those who do brain work all day might find satisfaction in carpentry, cooking, or raking autumn leaves. Some in caregiving professions, which can take heavy emotional tolls, benefit from early morning exercise workouts, mountain climbing, water sports, and other physical activities. The best ways to feed our body and soul are a combination of the things we enjoy most and from which we receive satisfaction.

Doing the best we can, with what we have, where we are, will always guarantee that every day will be rewarding, even exhilarating, despite any setbacks we may face. It's the small pleasures, the smiles, the satisfactions, the kind words, and the encouragement we give others that add to a rich and fulfilling life. As your soul expands, everything around you increases in value.

> *"WHATEVER YOU ARE PHYSICALLY...MALE OR FEMALE, STRONG OR WEAK, ILL OR HEALTHY—ALL THOSE THINGS MATTER LESS THAN WHAT YOUR HEART CONTAINS. IF YOU HAVE THE SOUL OF A WARRIOR, YOU ARE A WARRIOR. ALL THOSE OTHER THINGS, THEY ARE THE GLASS THAT CONTAINS THE LAMP, BUT YOU ARE THE LIGHT INSIDE."*
>
> — CASSANDRA CLARE, CLOCKWORK ANGEL

CHAPTER 6

Our Endless Spirit

ACCORDING TO C.S. Lewis, "You are never too old to set another goal or to dream a new dream." The spirit that you and I received at birth will remain with us as long as we live on earth, and is the only part of us that will live eternally. Few of us realize that we are a living spirit and mind housed in a human body, and created in the image and likeness of God. The human spirit instilled in each of us at birth is the eternal bond that unites us with our Creator. It is that ineffable, immeasurable, priceless element in each man, woman, and child who lives that came as a gift at the time of our birth. It is the spiritual power that fuels the hopes and desires that dwell within us. It motivates us to aspire, think beyond our human boundaries, and follow the ideas and aspirations that often seem beyond our human reach. No one can adequately describe this dynamic spiritual attribute that resides within us. Our spirit is something we should cherish as the Holy Grail within our life. It is not something to ignore, as too many people do, but to revere as the most priceless possession we will ever have. President Ronald Reagan said:

> *"THERE ARE NO CONSTRAINTS ON THE HUMAN MIND, NO WALLS AROUND THE HUMAN SPIRIT, NO BARRIERS TO OUR PROGRESS EXCEPT THOSE WE OURSELVES ERECT."*

When we do our best with what we have each day, no matter how simple or mundane the tasks, we expand our capacities and increase our abilities. Doing the best we can, to the highest degree possible at the moment means far more than mechanistic progress or egotistical accomplishment. By doing the best we can with what we have, to the fullest of our ability, all the time, will enable us, by degrees, to become all we are humanly capable of being. As a divinely created three-dimensional being, we must learn how to synchronize our mind, body, and spirit for maximum utilization. John C. Maxwell said:

"ENJOYMENT IS AN INCREDIBLE ENERGIZER TO THE HUMAN SPIRIT."

Most people need to learn how to enjoy themselves and their life. Certain periods of any life seem to offer little hope for finding any enjoyment among the drab routines and endless rounds of hard work. I can certainly relate to this, thanks to the many years of hard labor on our family farm during my early boyhood. Those endless days of drudgery seemed to cost too much at the time, but it was from those experiences that I learned to appreciate the nobility of hard work and thankless tasks such as plowing fields, planting crops, cutting and stacking endless cords of wood for cooking and heating, and dealing with my struggles in muddy pigpens. Something inherent within us has the capacity to lift our thoughts above our earthly tasks. At times such as these, I found companionship in the star-filled heavens at night, the endlessness of celestial eternity, and the tracks of rabbits and deer in the freshly fallen snow.

Like countless other earthbound souls, I had to learn early in life that we must overcome our limitations and find ways to climb higher as we develop and mature. There's something within us that must go further, that must go higher to reach the peaks of our capacities. In May 1953, Sir Edmund Hillary, with Tenzing Norgay, became the first to reach the pinnacle of the world's highest mountain. Mount Everest reaches 29,035 feet. Previously, only Sherpas attained that height and the news made Hillary and his companion worldwide celebrities. Sir Hillary modestly professed not to understand the furor. He said:

"YOU DON'T HAVE TO BE A FANTASTIC HERO TO DO CERTAIN THINGS—TO COMPETE. YOU CAN BE JUST AN ORDINARY CHAP, SUFFICIENTLY MOTIVATED TO REACH CHALLENGING GOALS."

Dr. Norman Vincent Peale often told audiences about the word "enthusiasm," which comes from the Greek *en theos*, meaning God within. He believed and often preached on the importance of enthusiasm within the human spirit. A Georgia housewife told of reading an article which declared enthusiasm to be 80 percent of success. As a stay-at-home mother of three young children, the woman felt trapped among a welter of repetitive tasks and endless questions, demands, and mishaps. She loved her household full of so much life, but longed for what she called "a life of my own."

Thinking about enthusiasm, she said, made all the difference. She decided to enjoy everything she could about her offspring's early childhoods. Meanwhile, she would study herself and her desires and make positive plans for what she could do when her children reached school age. The approach worked. Not only did she learn to enjoy and take great satisfaction in her brilliant children, but in later years each felt the same way about their mother.

"I discovered I was an entrepreneur," she said. "First I became a fashion model for several department stores. I enjoyed that, but enjoyed even more opening a tea room and catering business. I began speaking to women's groups and later studied finance and investing." All this happened because she absorbed the full meaning of one word: enthusiasm.

As a man of the Christian faith, I believe strongly and have learned many lessons about how normal it is for a Spirit Power to direct our daily activities and how easily we can connect our mind and thoughts to the Spiritual power of our Creator. Many people believe this and connect with it during their journey through life, and somehow become eager for new ideas and more sophisticated outlooks that their faith once knew and seldom remembered. Perhaps a crisis occurs and the person wonders if God is real. This is one's opportunity to ask a question in truth and mean it.

Often I counsel individuals who years earlier ceased to believe in a Creator who would allow injustice, abuse, and every other sort of human evil to happen. As individuals, we were given free will, and the ability to choose how we desired to live. When bad things happen to even the best people, we seek possible answers and often find none. In our frustrating and often dysfunctional world, many people blame God for all that is evil and inhuman. God, however, created none of it. Just as He allows us to choose what is wrong, he offers us the opportunities to choose what is right. He gives us choices to improve our life and achieve our heart's desire. He gives us the freedom to become the person we were created to be. By doing the best we can with what we have, we learn to trust ourselves and strengthen our faith in God and ourselves. By reaching higher and seeing our aspirations take shape, we learn to trust God more as our mind and spirituality develop.

As we learn to trust our faith and ourselves, we become more intuitive and more sensitive to the unseen forces that govern our destiny. Each of us has had sudden impulses that seemed to make no sense, but later proved to be the reason we avoided physical harm or discovered greater opportunities. A woman I know related one of those strange stories to me:

"Dick is a business colleague who lived in New Jersey. From time to time, one of us would text or phone the other, but not on a regular basis. On this occasion, I really hadn't thought about Dick for a couple of years when I felt an urgency to contact him. I postponed phoning for a day, but the impulse continued, so I stopped what I was doing and made the call. I live in Florida and Dick lives in New Jersey, so I could hardly believe what he was telling me. I didn't realize they had ice and snow that time of the year, but in a panicky voice, he described being iced in, yet he had made the decision that he and his wife would drive to their office and work.

"He drove through snow and ice on empty roadways, and managed to reach their destination. Just as he opened the office door, his wife slipped and fell and broke her arm. Dick could not start their car, and in a strained voice asked me to pray because he didn't know what to do. I told him to call the State Patrol and take the scarf or muffler he was wearing and make a sling for her arm. The phone connection was bad and I wondered if he heard what I said. As I paced the floor, it occurred to me that I should call the New Jersey State Patrol and make sure the search was on."

My friend then prayed for a good outcome. That morning her friend Dick phoned to say they were helicoptered out only minutes later, that Brenda's arm had been properly set, and they were home. The strange thing he related was that his phone ran out of power before he could call the State Patrol, yet they arrived moments later. Was this a coincidence? Not for those who have these inner impulses and obey them. Such miracles happen every day. The most sensitive part of us, our wonderful and invisible conscious, flames highest and burns brightest at times it is most needed.

Something makes a man dive into a frozen lake to rescue a boy who fell through the ice. The man cannot explain why he spontaneously reacted. He did not think it through or imagine what it might cost him. He might always remember the incident and how he shrugged off peoples' reactions by saying, "I'm glad I was there," but if he lives, he will never understand the divine force that propelled his response. That force cannot be humanly understood nor can it be adequately described. The call to self-sacrifice, bravery, or heroism gets answered every hour of every day at some point in the world. In a world that often seems too dark, too unholy, or too brutal to endure, it is good to look to every inspirational circumstance to reassure ourselves that if God's Eternal Spirit exists, our spirit can reach that of our Creator.

Simple things can inspire us. I like to walk the two-and-a-half miles to my office each morning. This time of day brings certain sights, scents, and sounds from the woods behind my home and the river beyond. I may see a deer gazing at me or a red fox strolling to his morning work of finding food. There are pauses along the way to greet a small child and her dog or wave to a neighbor. The morning air awakens my senses and my walk becomes far more than exercise for my body, but a return to the riches of nature that I learned to appreciate as a boy on our farm in the northern woods of Minnesota. I often wonder where my red fox lives or if the deer will stay safe from the passing cars. Some of the birds seem to follow me as I compliment them for their well-chosen songs. There is so much in nature that fills my life with hopeful aspirations and noble inspirations.

On my return walk, the day is in full bloom and I sense fully the change in seasons. High summer is gone, grasses are beginning to brown, and the sky is a hazy blue that seems to lure one towards the hills to enjoy a full display of the red and gold splendor of the bushes and trees. These simple things, these spirit-lifting things, belong to each of us. Wherever we live in this world, we can find beauty and wonder and the glory of living things that populate the area in which we live. Our body, mind, and soul work together in ways far beyond our mortal understanding.

I have spoken of my difficult and circumscribed early life, which seemed to offer little chance to venture outside the fences of our farm. One amazing year when I was in my late teens, I won the 4-H National Citizenship Scholarship Award, and a trip to our Nation's capital. Mr. Thomas E. Wilson, my gracious sponsor, invited me to ride with him in his private Pullman car. I thanked Mr. Wilson and told him I had been given my plane ticket for the trip, but he insisted that I accompany him as he was my sponsor.

At age 18, I had never had a train ride, much less experienced such a trip in a luxurious private Pullman car. Neither had I ever flown in an airplane. I hesitated momentarily, but chose to accept Mr. Wilson's kind offer. As the long journey progressed, and my sponsor slept, I found myself conscious of the swaying of the train and a myriad of thoughts swirling around in my mind as I gazed into the night and wondered about the people who lived in the farm houses we passed as the train went by.

The trip was altogether memorable in every respect, as I recounted in my book, *Hope, Desire, and Aspire*. On returning, however, the series of glorious experiences ended abruptly when we reached Chicago. There we learned that the flight on which I was booked had crashed with no survivors. It seemed as if there was a power that guided our steps. Why had Mr. Wilson been so insistent that I travel with him on the train? So many questions never get answered. However, each life contains such episodes that cause us to wonder if God is protecting us for some special reason. Incidentally, though my later life has included too many flights to count, it happens that there was to be only one experience in a luxurious, private Pullman car.

As I have said, my wife and I have visited over 100 countries on every continent, including the South Pole and North Pole. My career has included long stretches of intense activity and innumerable challenges, including months that grew into years of separation. My wife worked equally hard within her family's candle business and her commitment to cultural causes. She wisely understood that as much as we needed time together, we needed to stretch our horizons as we established our individual businesses. It was Peggy who planned, researched, and worked out the logistics of each trip we took.

Together we discovered far more than new horizons, new adventures, and new knowledge. Again and again we learned the basic truth that in the world's myriad cultures, ethnicities, and beliefs, human beings of every rank, station, and degree of sophistication have a singular thing in common: the desire to be appreciated and respected and recognized as an individual. There is something within us that wants to break down barriers of mistrust, fear, and suspicion and bring about that spark of faith and humanity that unites us all with our Creator.

Each of us can elevate our expectations and develop and expand our spiritual attributes when we have found our purpose and believe it is our reason for being. In 1958, a runner by the name of Roger Bannister did what science called impossible when he broke the four-minute mile. The human body could not attain such a dangerous objective, it was argued. Bannister concentrated, visualized, practiced, and broke the world's record. In subsequent years, other runners followed and today even superbly trained high school athletes occasionally accomplish the same feat. As Bannister said:

"THE MAN WHO CAN DRIVE HIMSELF FURTHER ONCE THE EFFORT GETS PAINFUL IS THE MAN WHO WILL WIN."

What does your spirit desire? Are you willing to lift your limits? Are you willing to become all you are capable of being? Are you willing to do the best you can with what you have? Are you willing to believe in yourself? These are more than questions—these are statements of your potential. These are yours to answer by the way you live and the thoughts you allow to occupy your mind.

You are the only person on this earth that controls the course of your life. Others can help you and give you advice and make suggestions from which you can benefit, but only you can make the decisions that will determine who you become and what you accomplish. Your mind and your spirit, your attitude and your outlook, are the compass that guides you to the North Star of your life.

It is what you believe that determines who you become. The spirit that dwells within you is God's presence in your life. Ask and you shall receive, seek and you shall find, believe and you shall discover. It is all within you and your thoughts.

> *"NO PESSIMIST EVER DISCOVERED THE SECRET OF THE STARS, OR SAILED TO AN UNCHARTED LAND, OR OPENED A NEW DOORWAY FOR THE HUMAN SPIRIT."*
>
> *— HELEN KELLER*

CHAPTER 7

The Greatest Life Insurance

LEARNING TO DO the best we can with what we have is the finest and least expensive form of life insurance. The habit of doing our best cannot prevent the trials and tribulations that happen in most of our lives, but it does guarantee a level of intentional striving towards excellence that enlarges and strengthens our character and our ability to become the person we are capable of being. Each of our lives is part of a greater life. The more we become, and the more consistent and dependable we become, the more our finer qualities and character develop in the process.

Doing all we can do to the best of our ability day after day strengthens the qualities of our character and increases the capacities of our ability. When the ill winds of life blow across our personal life and nothing seems to prosper, when we look ahead to seasons of hardship and loss, the habit of doing the best we can, despite the circumstances that surround us, provides the hope, persistence, and perseverance that ultimately proves this too will pass.

I recall reading a newspaper article shortly after the Vietnam War began about a hardware store owner and his wife whose two sons entered military service and were shipped abroad. Not only did the store owner lose his two assistants, but those young men were his only sons and were now in harm's way. As the months progressed and the news worsened, the man's concerns were heightened when a big box store moved into his neighborhood. It seemed that he might lose his business. The neighborhood was changing, fewer people came in to buy his merchandise, and the man's fears mounted. Not only might he lose one or both of his boys, but it seemed inevitable that he would lose his store as well.

The owner and his wife did their best, but there seemed to be little relief for their concerns. One morning he woke up with a strong and urgent feeling that he should paint the interior of his store. He could not afford to hire a painter, and re-arranging his stock and shelves presented a daunting task. However, the thought would not leave his mind. It seemed pointless to paint the walls of a place he might be losing, but he couldn't rid himself of the feeling it must be done. After several days of internal struggle, he stayed an extra couple of hours after closing, moving numerous items, and preparing the first wall. The next morning he arrived very early and painted until the first customer came in. The work was slow and difficult, but the few customers who came in praised his efforts, saying, "This place will look great when you finish painting." As days of hard work progressed, the owner conceived ways to better showcase his stock.

"There was so much toting and carrying, bending and stretching, that my body stayed sore for weeks," he said, but he could not overcome a growing sense of excitement and expectation. "Neighbors came in," he said, "probably out of curiosity, but friendships were renewed over cups of coffee and offers of help," and eventually he was back in business.

"I'm convinced this work was an answer to prayer," he said. "It didn't seem to make sense at first, but I followed my feelings and it worked. Thankfully, both of our boys returned safe and helped me with the business, which is progressing as never before. We are grateful and thankful."

Such examples of acting when it seems there is no reason to act or any possibility of a good outcome, offer hope and inspiration to all of us. A housewife has a recipe for what to do when she feels overwhelmed:

"I scrub or polish a floor," she said. "You see great results immediately, and one activity leads to the next. Pretty soon you have made enough headway that you can confidently expect to handle the rest of the stuff that's piling on."

The habit of doing all that we can with what we have leads us to a greater, more productive work ethic. Some people's performance is so unproductive that you scarcely want to hire them. A woman rushed into a ladies' luncheon late, explaining that she had just come from her son's apartment, which had been burglarized.

"All his electronic equipment was stolen and detectives said they had never seen a place in such disarray," she laughed. "It's his first apartment and it looks like a junkyard," she explained. "His girlfriend comes on Saturdays and helps with laundry and tries to tidy, but it's hopeless. I keep my mouth shut," she said, "because the only important thing is he's doing outstanding work at his first job."

The problem with that explanation is that eventually sloppiness in one area leads to difficulties in the next. If the young man's car looks like his dwelling, no doubt it creates a negative impression. It's like the corporate executive who boasted to a business owner colleague that his IT specialist could no doubt help solve an expansion problem for the other man's business.

"He's a genius," the first man bragged. "He can offer you at least two or three possibilities for great, low-cost solutions."

The computer genius was called in, politely offered three ideas that seemed sound, but the businessman seemed reluctant. "I take your word that this guy is brilliant, and he seems to be, but somehow I find it hard to bet the future of my company on the word of a guy whose socks don't match."

These stories sound humorous but are actually costly answers of specializing in areas natural and easy and ignoring seemingly unimportant details. As Dillon Burroughs, author of *Thirst No More: A One-Year Devotional Journey*, said:

"MUCH OF LIFE APPEARS MUNDANE AT THE TIME. YET IN GOD'S PROVIDENCE EVERY MOMENT INCLUDES SIGNIFICANT DETAILS ARRANGED BY HIS DIVINE HAND."

In today's knowledge-based world, where work and careers often leapfrog from one success to the next, often there's little incentive to consider the architecture of our lives. Doing the best we can with what we have is our daily challenge and greatest opportunity. To focus on what is easy and comfortable, to delight in our major talents and ignore our weaknesses, often precedes our failed efforts. Management experts will point out that too much success too early in life usually leads to business and personal failure, because of over-confidence and lack of proven ability.

If we do the best we can with what we have in every aspect of our life, we will ensure our success as much as possible. The more we succeed, the more success and substance will become a measurable part of our life. This will hold true in all phases of life, because results speak louder than intentions or well-spoken words. The significant part of this equation is that such lives will become positive examples for those with whom they associate. Children learn a great deal by observing others. The adult who exhibits good character and high work ethics invariably inspires others to do their best. Good work is contagious. We know it when we see it and it creates the desire within us to improve our efforts and our surroundings.

I shall never forget the influence I had on the street where I first lived in Little Rock, Arkansas. It was a poor neighborhood where all the houses were small and drab with unkempt yards. The first thing I did when I moved in was paint the house and improve the yard. I never spoke of what I was doing or the reason I did what I did. But within less than a year, every house on the street was repainted and the yards were improved. One of the greatest lessons I learned was the fact that we are the examples of who we are, and what we do becomes the proof of what we represent.

When we speak of true insurance we are speaking of more than financial security, we are speaking of mental, cultural, social, and personal security which is determined by the way we live and the influence we have on those who know us. Used in this sense, we want our life's journey to offer us as much meaningful lifetime success and security as possible. To accomplish this objective, we must invest as much of ourselves and our abilities as possible in everything we do, thus initiating the example others will recognize, and hopefully encourage them to do their best as well. Unfortunately, many who seek comfort are often among those who seek to achieve without giving and receive without effort. They are some of the most numerous users of pain medications and other artificial tranquilizers. Avoiding pain at any cost has too often become a habit for thousands of individuals whose ideas and talents could enrich the world if properly used. Once such people become energized by those with more creative visions, even the most hopeless and useless lives can be changed.

The insurance policy I am describing will steadily increase in value and substantially increase your life's prosperity. This can mean greater wealth over time, in terms of financial, cultural, and intellectual qualities. However, prosperity in its overall sense includes health, well-being, respect, achievement, generosity, and many other intangibles. It includes a life of thanksgiving, even in times of misfortune or grief. It means gratitude for one's ability to care for others, to offer physical, mental, or emotional help in times of trouble. Prosperity means overflowing and fulfilling. Anyone can increase the value of their life if they will do the best they can with what they have.

A tornado ripped through a dairy farm one Christmas Eve, destroying buildings, livestock, and scattering implements over great distances. This was one of the most prosperous dairy farms in the region, utterly destroyed. At first light on Christmas morning, men and women came from all directions to help the distressed farmer. Wounded animals had to be destroyed and carcasses removed. The few surviving cows and calves were loaded into trucks and carried to neighboring barns. Shattered lumber and destruction went as far as the eye could see, but all day people worked, trucks rolled, food was cooked, gallons of coffee were brewed, and with few words spoken, as much as could be done was done. The hardware store opened so tools could be obtained. There were no tears shed by the farm family, because there was no time to grieve, only to move as fast as hands and feet could to deliver whatever was needed by those who wanted to help by doing their best.

The rest of the story demonstrates the highest and best that lives in the hearts of good, solid people. The barn was rebuilt, larger and stronger than the one destroyed. People donated nails, boards, and tools, and everyone worked as a team. One day a truck rolled up from Amish country with a gift of two prize cows. Others contributed livestock as well. When all was finished, the farmer had the finest barn and buildings, plus the best herd of dairy cattle in the county.

What does this show? It shows that doing all that we can is not done only for ourselves but for others as well. In the same spirit, we transmit our convictions and core values to our friends and associates in the spirit of generosity and compassion. In this way, a community of citizens contributed the best of themselves to one of their own. Is it fair, someone asked, that this farmer should come out ahead of all the others? Not as men perceive fairness, perhaps, but so indicative of the grace of God, which mere men and women so often express when they do all they can for the benefit of others.

> ***"I THINK…IF IT IS TRUE THAT THERE ARE AS MANY MINDS AS THERE ARE HEADS, THEN THERE ARE AS MANY KINDS OF LOVE AS THERE ARE HEARTS."***
>
> Leo Tolstoy, *Anna Karenina*

I submit that doing all you can with what you have leads to peace, contentment, and satisfaction. It certainly contributes to peace in one's heart when it leads to compassion for others. Our trials and tribulations may differ, but in many ways they are much the same. When we learn to do the best we can with what we have, to solve our problems regardless of size, we increase our ability to surmount each crisis that comes our way. We were created to be independent and interdependent; we were created to give and to share, to be and become as we develop into the person we were born to be. Our peace and well-being contributes to our family and friends, our workplace, and the world in which we live. Think of what is best for you and the life you live: to be all you can be, to encourage and support, to love and to share, to inspire and reassure, to be a faithful friend and trusted confidant. To do unto others as you would have them do unto you.

Doing all we can with what we have makes the silent statement, "I am responsible. I care about you as well as myself." As President Harry S. Truman famously said, "The buck stops here." To become responsible means I am "response-able." It means I intend to offer everything I am to the task or challenge at hand, and by doing so, I become increasingly able to accept greater responsibilities and greater opportunities. This personal and remarkable insurance policy offers families, businesses, and communities the kind of human security that each of us needs.

The True-Life Insurance, as described above, promotes good mental and physical health, as brain and muscles are used to ever-increasing benefit. Study the lives of people who live well into their nineties and beyond, and you will see a pattern of healthy decision making, consistent follow-through, and overall success. Such people are heartier than most. I suggest that they have given more to life than many others give, and have received not only more longevity but far greater satisfaction. These folks are not loners, but friends to many. One centenarian lady in a nursing home wrote two newspaper columns per week and corresponded with dozens of friends around the world.

"I wrote letters to people my age and now correspond with their children, grandchildren, and great-grandchildren," she laughed. She was a colorful piece of humanity and dozens of friends lived, laughed, and learned alongside a woman who possessed the world's best and truest life insurance policy.

As Dr. Albert Schweitzer, the noted minister, missionary, author, and musician, opined: "We should have reverence for life." The noted doctor served in Africa well into his old age, doing a number of things with the utmost ability. His secret was that of working at construction until he tired, then practicing the organ for an hour, moving on into writing or studying, then returning to gardening, and so forth. His rich life and great wisdom was expressed through seemingly ordinary tasks that inspired people in Africa and around the world. Reverence for life is a by-product of what we do with our lives, or perhaps the other way around. It can and should be a foundation for our life, no matter how ordinary we perceive ourselves to be. Reverence for life includes all creatures besides ourselves, a never-ending chain of the Creator's creations.

A friend of mine leads a life of similar excellence and versatility. Dr. Hamilton Dixon, who I have known for 20 years, at age 82 sees patients four days a week. At least five days a week, he practices piano for two hours each day. He continually adds additional works to his classical repertoire, and gives a public concert once a year. Dr. Dixon is best known for his world-class rowing skills.

At age seven, when he began learning to play the piano, he also began to model the sort of personal discipline he saw in his father. "My father was a genius, a poet, a Shakespearean scholar who could recite all the poet's sonnets from memory. I saw my father pursue everything he did with the utmost in excellence, and from this I learned to compete." When Hamilton completed high school in two and one-half years, he said "I had no time for sports, nor was I interested." When he entered college he weighed 145 pounds, was 6'3" tall, and soon was approached by the rowing coach who announced that Dixon would join the rowing team.

The experience was an epiphany for him, one that not only caused him to develop into a 185-pound, well-muscled athlete by the time he graduated, but he began a lifetime of passion for the sport. Whether in perfectly synchronized eight-man races, a four-man team, a double, or in a single skull, to date Hamilton has won over 101 gold and silver medals all over the country, plus five world championships from 2006-2010 on the Concept 2 rowing machine, now a worldwide sport that comes to Boston every January. "My goal is to continue rowing until I'm 100," he declares. Dr. Dixon's well-balanced lifestyle enhances every aspect of his existence, as each activity seems to nourish the next. He was knighted in England in 1988 in the field of Humanities.

He enjoys his medical practice and the fact that Jane, his wife of 61 years, has worked alongside him so they can be together every day. His years of physical exercise and constantly improved skills have kept his physical body as energetic and well performing as that of a much younger man. His weight remains a healthy 185 pounds, and his upper body strength and dexterity provide the perfect apparatus for performing bravura passages on his nine-foot-long concert grand piano. Playing the piano is known to be a superb brain challenge, since using both hands simultaneously exercises both sides of the human brain.

This man's fascinating life illustrates how successfully one's mind, will, emotions, and physical body can each contribute to the next. No wonder Dr. Dixon, whose medical age could be estimated to be 60, can hope to continue his lifestyle to the 100-year mark. His modest personality makes it difficult to learn much about his extraordinary successes, but Hamilton Dixon exudes joy when he speaks of his wife, their five children, sixteen grandchildren, and six great-grandchildren. What is this patriarch's legacy to his large clan? One grandson, already an avid oarsman with awards to his credit, was accepted into Harvard University and is beginning his senior year. "I believe he will become an Olympic oarsman," his grandfather said.

The significance of a life lived this fully with an aim toward competing well, performing well, and experiencing the richness of life's natural and manmade beauty, bestows examples of excellence and joy that go far beyond the ripples on any river. The wonderful thing is each of us can have that kind of life, one overflowing with extraordinary experiences.

From time to time our soul cries out for more, some nameless thing that lies beyond us. When we do all that we can do, we step into a channel of blessings which leads us beyond ourselves, into the community of life with all mankind.

> *"I AM COME THAT THEY MIGHT HAVE LIFE AND THAT THEY MIGHT HAVE IT MORE ABUNDANTLY."*
>
> —JESUS

Part Two: With What You Have

If you count all your assets you always show a profit.

WILSON MIZNER

CHAPTER 8

The Assets You Possess

BY DOING THE best you can with what you have, you will increase all you possess. Many people come to me for counseling at times when they are experiencing great personal or financial losses, or believe their lives, in some respect, have failed. The truth is if we will evaluate all the tangible and intangible assets we own, we will understand how much more we have than we realize. You may object to this assertion, but it's true. There is much we possess in terms of experience, ideas, information, and knowledge that we have gained in the process of living than we can imagine.

Each of us is a unique individual, created with an enormously complex and abundant potential of capacities, such as talent, ability, creativity, vision, aspiration, and emotional energy. If our lives were like a bank account, we could see the continuing, creative, and productive deposits we make through our experiences and achievements. Every positive effort and every creative thought increases the value of our experience and the knowledge gained in the process of doing whatever we have done. To be fair, our life demands withdrawals as well, but my statement remains positive—what we have now is all that we need now. What we have is an abundance of experience that enables us to achieve what we can achieve **now**.

I think of a famous and well-beloved entertainer who visited with me in my office at a time of great personal crisis. She enumerated her failures, some due to her own mistakes, and others far beyond her control. As she placed blame upon herself again and again, I saw how much her self-condemnation was overwhelming this lovely and talented woman.

That day I gave her an assignment: "Go home and list on a piece of paper every positive asset you possess. You are young, talented, beautiful, and intelligent. Start with those," I said, "and you will see how much you have to be grateful for, and the blessings you have in your talents and natural beauty."

She turned her teary eyes to me and said, "Intelligent? I'm stupid or I would not be in this mess."

Interestingly, most people who have come to me for counsel say much the same thing. They've made a mistake, lost a business or a marriage, encountered failure for the first time, and found it overwhelming. They labeled themselves with the word "failure," a false assumption. It often takes months, even years, for such individuals to gain a more balanced and justified opinion of themselves. I have observed that most of us are far more compassionate to our neighbors and friends than we are towards ourselves, whereas God forgives all who come to Him in their time of need. It is not our position to judge; it is our position to encourage and support.

The entertainer I mentioned had to ask a close friend to help her see anything worthwhile in her sadly stricken life. She thought and wrote for hours the first day and continued the assignment of valuation for a week, before she handed me the pages of her life's assets. Then I mentioned the word "friends" to her, because she was beloved internationally. "Too many to list," she said, laughing at the absurdity of her belief that she had nothing to live for and nothing to hope for.

In the following years, with a succession of ups and downs, this beautiful and talented woman has discovered a new purpose, a new fruitfulness, and a high sense of divine calling. What she lost by her self-condemnation has not been totally restored, but her soul has been enriched and her passion for life has been recovered. She has found her purpose.

Dr. John C. Maxwell, noted author and trainer of individuals in leadership, wrote *Failing Forward*, a best-selling book which describes the uses of failure. Whereas most people see failure as negative, Dr. Maxwell and I agree that often failure closes one of life's doors so that we will reassess our position and choose another path to follow.

I feel certain that most readers at this moment are not dealing with failure issues. However, if each of us were to list our personal assets, we would quickly realize we were living far beneath our potential. Consider the word "genius," which we apply to such legendary figures as Albert Einstein or Steve Jobs. Both gentlemen probably possessed above-average intelligence quotients, as many of the rest of us do, but for years science has told us we are each using slightly more than ten percent of our intelligence. Could it be that those willing to exert their curiosity, imagination, or willingness to pursue knowledge, simply go beyond the ten percent?

What if each of us took the brain power that was given to us at birth, and decided to expand it in the pursuit of our individual calling? Those who decide to do all they can with what they have will find that their talents and abilities continually increase as they are used. As they utilize the talents they have to the best of their ability, they increase their mentality and capability, and two factors will emerge: what they have added to what they have done has increased their experience and expanded their capacity to improve upon what they have done before. This is the way those who succeed become more successful.

The greatest asset we can possess is a noble character based upon our integrity and loving compassion. Doing all we can with what we have day after day will produce an honest, stable, dependable, and enviable reputation. These intangible qualities will enable a worthy person to reach the pinnacle of a worthy life. Without them, the most brilliant and talented individuals inevitably will fall short of their potential.

Many of the stories you read in this book will illustrate the two principles outlined above. A small example comes to mind. A young woman beginning a new sales career loved her job, except for the often strenuous travel, and like others on the sales team, the hated monthly expense account. When she assessed those two problems, she realized she didn't mind days of long hours and unpredictable travel, but the fact she had to keep records of mileage and expenses was what she really hated. Like other members of the team, she constantly complained about the mountain of accumulated receipts and the need to keep accurate records. She did all she could with the problem by keeping a daily calendar, which included names, dates, places, mileage, and even gratuities.

She offered that printout to her sales manager, along with the receipts organized by date. In her effort to do all she could, an ironic inspiration came to her: she purchased glossy pocket folders, inserted her business card in the slot, placed her printout on one side and receipts on the other, and handed the handsome package to her boss.

"You don't need to go to this much trouble," her boss remarked, but obviously liked her complete and perfect report, so different from the handful of crumpled receipts other team members offered him. In time her idea of doing all she could made her most disagreeable task much easier. The fact that she made her manager's job much easier was a bonus. This win-win solution was possibly the reason she was soon given greater responsibility, a wider territory, and a much larger salary.

What we often have may seem less than we desire, like a handful of crumpled receipts, or opportunities or events that never seem to be fulfilled. Countless true stories emerge each day of people whose early lives seemed hopeless as they struggled to make a living, yet a moment came when they realized they had enough within themselves to make a new beginning. Earlier, I told of a financially wealthy young man who realized on his 40th birthday that he needed to rebuild his life because it was physically and emotionally going downhill. It is not always money that we need, but often the honest realization that an aspect of our character is lacking, or that we refuse to accept opportunities freely available to us.

There is an old saying that goes: "Water seeks its own level." Too many people fail to do their best or expect more than they are willing to give of themselves or their efforts. Those who go the "extra mile" and do far more than is expected, those people like Steve Jobs who appear perhaps once in a century, are willing to venture beyond themselves by doing all they possibly can with what they have. These are the people who change the world because they keep on trying to achieve their vision, until it ultimately becomes a reality. These are the people who believe in themselves and are secure in the knowledge of their abilities.

As for Dr. Albert Einstein, that famous professor of physics and author of the theory of relativity, there's a humorous story concerning a newspaper reporter who asked Einstein's wife if she understood her husband's famous theory.

"No, but I know how he likes his tea," she responded.

Here was a woman as secure in her own calling as much as her genius husband was secure in his. No person is inherently less than others and no man or woman created in the image of God can possibly be insignificant. We all have a potential that is worthy of respect, but we must each become worthy of our own potential.

One of the most fascinating stories of self-assessment concerns a businessman named Peter J. Daniels, reputedly one of the wealthiest men in Australia. At age 26, Daniels was a third-generation welfare recipient, illiterate, with several family members incarcerated. He worked as a brick layer and, except for that job, obviously had little in his life to list as assets. One night he attended a Billy Graham evangelistic crusade and for the first time heard a startling truth: "God is no respecter of persons." This fact revolutionized the young man's thinking.

As he began using what he had by overcoming illiteracy, utilizing his heretofore unrecognized intelligence, and doing all he could with what he had, Daniels eventually became an extraordinary developer and businessman with holdings in Australia and Asia. He wrote more than 20 books, has given more than 1,000 seminars worldwide, and holds positions on many international boards. When you read his best-selling books or his Internet biography, you will be amazed at what can emerge from a life that apparently began with nothing.

If you believe, as I believe, that there are untold thousands of failures who could succeed, if they removed their self-imposed limitations, and radically change the world in which we all live. Perhaps you are overly aware of your own limitations and focus your thoughts on what you haven't accomplished. In my 50 years of counseling individuals, both prominent and little known, concerning their perceived position in society, I have come to realize we are unlimited, except for limits we place on ourselves. Think for a moment and recall some of the stories you've heard about:

- *A quadriplegic woman who has written best-selling books and helped countless physically disabled individuals go forward in life.*
- *A tournament-winning golfer who was blind.*
- *A ballet dancer who could not hear the music but felt its vibration beneath her feet.*
- *A paralyzed man who became an American President.*

There are similar stories too numerous to count. Undeniably, Helen Keller, a blind, mute, and deaf child, showed the world how to see and hear far more than most of us ever learn to do. The little girl, struck down by a severe illness in early childhood, had to be taught how to communicate, how to talk intelligently, how to learn without vision or sound and, most of all, how to overcome losses unimaginable to most of us. Helen Keller became one of the best-educated and wisest thinkers of the 20th century. Her spirit proved that we human beings have been created to become creators and are built to become achievers.

Our human liabilities often inhibit this process unnecessarily. Excuses cancel opportunities for success:

- *I don't feel like it.*
- *That's not my job.*
- *I get no help from anybody.*
- *I'm not paid to do that.*
- *I never had a chance.*
- *That's beyond my pay grade.*

These excuses remove countless thousands from any chance of prosperity. Of course, this reflects our individual choices as to whether we go forward or stand still and regress. It is not only a personal decision, but one that affects all of us. Other negative attributes include blaming others for our own failures, anger, jealousy, fear, a desire to get even, and similar mental and emotional traits that diminish the possibilities of success. Whatever is negative will prove destructive and diminish our potential for success. Whatever is positive will enhance our ability to succeed and prosper.

Among our greatest assets and opportunities is our freedom to choose the course we take and the purpose for which we live. Too often I hear people say, "I have run out of options" or "It's my fault.

I messed up my life and it can't be helped." Such statements are inaccurate, self-fulfilling, and insulting to the Creator who gave us life. At any point in our life, even at our lowest, we can decide to do all we can do to overcome the obstacles we face. There is power in struggle and determination in commitment. We encourage others by the example we establish.

When Peter Daniels realized he was qualified to become more than he believed he was, year by year as he did more with what he had, he became more of what he was destined to become. He is a world-famous businessman, yet three times he failed at business. Never did he declare bankruptcy, however, but just began again and each time he climbed higher. Among his many gifts and successes has been that of inviting untold thousands who read his books and hear his lectures to turn to God who created them and ask for His purpose for their lives. Time and again when I saw no way of succeeding, I would ask God to show me the way.

Every noble achievement, every beautiful work of art, every great book, fantastic building, or majestic symphony, had its beginning in the mind and thoughts of a single individual. Focus your thoughts on the powers you possess, and the means of releasing those powers for the benefit of others will become clear to you. The assets within you as a person are important to all who know you. When you show others you are interested in them, they will respond with their respect and support.

> *TRUST YOURSELF. CREATE THE KIND OF SELF THAT YOU WILL BE HAPPY TO LIVE WITH ALL YOUR LIFE. MAKE THE MOST OF YOURSELF BY FANNING THE TINY, INNER SPARKS OF POSSIBILITY INTO FLAMES OF ACHIEVEMENT.*
>
> —GOLDA MEIR

CHAPTER 9

The Power of Vision

ONE OF OUR greatest assets is the ability to visualize what we desire to achieve. A vision is a divinely creative skill which offers us the opportunity to see the possibilities of what we can accomplish. Visions have inspired and motivated most of my major efforts. A vision, small or large, defines and stimulates an important objective, or an exciting task that may seem beyond our present abilities. When we do the best we can with what we have, with a vision of what we hope to accomplish, the inspiration our vision creates increases our capacity to achieve the outcome we desire. The power of our creative thoughts reside within the emotional energy our vision inspires. We are often surprised by the images that enter our mind, as we visualize the possibilities of our creative thoughts. Nothing is more exciting than a vision that contains the many possibilities of its realization.

The visualization process is both simple and complex. Our minds enable us to create in form and structure the vision we perceive as desirable. When Roger Bannister decided to pursue his vision of running a mile in under four minutes, an idea physicians and scientists called impossible, he nevertheless went forward. Bannister said he imagined that feat in every detail and held the possibility firmly in his mind.

As most sports trainers teach, the golfer must see the swing connecting perfectly with the small white ball, and feel the force of the club as it sends the ball toward its target. All this requires intense visualization: feeling each muscular action, the impact of the club against the ball, the feel of the swing, the sight of the ball rolling across the green, and so on.

At the end of a final quarter, a team member is called to kick a football over a goal post to win the game. It's a matter of the shoe perfectly connecting with an oblong ball which spirals into the air and continues to lift until at last it arcs above the goalpost. If the kicker could not feel his shoe against the pigskin, the muscles in his body acting in perfect coordination, or actively visualize the football's trajectory, would the result be the same? Most of us understand these concepts, but too few of us use them.

Throughout my professional career, I saw how creating visions inspired others to achieve the fulfillment of our objectives. Communities were changed and people were changed, because they saw what they could do when they were inspired to look beyond what had been done before. A vision is hope exemplified in a way that inspires tangible results.

A woman in Savannah, Georgia, looked out her window one day and saw children walking to school without any books in their hands. Annie Plummer loved books and words, and the sight of children with no books hurt her heart.

"I just couldn't understand it," she said. "How can a child go to school without books?"

Known not only in Savannah but throughout the country for passing out dictionaries to young children, Plummer started the project back in 1992. Her efforts expanded as publishers and others donated dictionaries, until thousands of local schoolchildren possessed the understanding of words to enjoy and live by.

Inside each dictionary, Plummer wrote: "A mind is a terrible thing to waste. I challenge you not to waste yours."

Plummer's efforts were mirrored across the country when similar programs began in Chicago, San Diego, and New Rochelle, New York, through the help of her family and friends.

In the beginning, when Annie Plummer saw the possibility of giving a few children dictionaries, she could not have imagined how much her vision would grow as she made more and more efforts to acquire and inscribe those books. Ultimately, she enlarged the minds of thousands of youngsters in her hometown and lived to see her vision spread far beyond her fondest dreams. Visions are useless without commitment and devotion. No worthy objective is ever too small, if one life can be changed for the better.

Inspiration such as Annie Plummer's leads to active visualization which, combined with prayer, can create results beyond our imagining. It is our faith in what we believe that inspires others to follow our leading. Our vision, inspired by our belief, helps us overcome discouragement due to failures or disappointments. Our sense of purpose defines and enlarges our vision and motivates our efforts. The honest and fruitful desires of our soul creates the capacity to achieve our highest expectations. Time and time again we can accomplish what was thought impossible because it had not been done before.

A Utah woman often gazed out her picture window and wished there were a tree somewhere in her large yard. She often said, "Children should have trees to climb." When her children were nearly grown, she had expressed the same wish so often that her husband brought home a tree and planted it exactly where she wanted it to be. Their children laughed and ridiculed the small tree their father had planted, but he continued to water and fertilize it, while ignoring their kidding.

Today the children's father has passed into the next life, but their grandchildren now climb the tree their grandmother long ago envisioned, as she watches from the picture window. Her desire might have seemed small, but in her mind's eye she saw the tree and the future generations that would climb as its branches expanded. The act of tree planting holds many practical and spiritual implications. As Martin Luther declared:

"EVEN IF I KNEW THAT TOMORROW THE WORLD WOULD GO TO PIECES, I WOULD STILL PLANT MY APPLE TREES."

Men have held this thought and acted upon it for centuries. On May 14, 1948, when the Nation of Israel was reborn, the land was one of sand dunes and desert. Among the first things the new settlers envisioned was that of planting trees and productive farms. Most farmers might have called this situation nearly hopeless, due to the hot sun, searing winds, and lack of water for irrigation. Despite those factors, the vision persisted. Visitors to the Holy Land often donated trees, a kibbutz soon learned ways to produce vegetables and fruits, and within a few short decades Israel had become one of the world's main exporters of fruits and flowers. Because of a people's vision, ways to irrigate were discovered, greenhouses were built, and today the desert blooms like a rose.

The way we visualize and what we visualize affects each day of our lives. Some look at what they have and see very little opportunity because of existing conditions. More often in prosperous times they see no need to use what they have for any purpose beyond themselves. Such people become victims of selfishness and impoverished imaginations. As Benjamin Franklin said:

"NECESSITY IS THE MOTHER OF INVENTION."

If this is true, we can find countless ways someone's needs have engendered a productive, new vision. In fact, as Henry Kaiser, the father of American shipbuilding said, "Find a need and fill it."

Visualization leads to actualization. In an article, Aymeric Guillot, Ph.D., a professor at the Center of Research and Innovation in Sports at University Claude Bernard Lyon in France, was quoted as saying, "Scientists believe that we may experience real-world and imaginary actions in similar ways." The article goes on: "He explained…whether we walk on a mountain trail or only picture it, we activate many of the same neural networks—paths of interconnected nerve cells that link what your body does to the brain impulses that control it. You can use this to your advantage in different ways. For example, imagining yourself doing movements can help you get better at them. Legendary golfer Jack Nicklaus practiced each shot in his mind before taking it."

The article quoted many examples of visualization, as we have mentioned above. "Arnold Schwarzenegger imagined his biceps to be mountain peaks as he pumped iron. Research has shown that surgeons, musicians, and business executives have used it to focus and to improve their performance."

This has been echoed countless times by others with entrepreneurial vision. Atlanta real estate developer, Thomas G. Cousins, one of two visionaries credited with changing Atlanta's skyline, created more visionary projects than we can describe here. As a developer who loved his hometown and enjoyed seeing her thrive, he constantly dreamed of ways of making his city prosper. For example, he envisioned restoring the neglected East Lake golf course, home of famed Grand Slam champion Bobby Jones. From that vision he drew investors into the idea of restoring surrounding housing and business areas. Thus, Purpose Built Communities was born and became a model for other such communities in New Orleans and Indianapolis. Not only were properties upgraded, but Cousins was proud of the hundreds of jobs created.

When a reporter asked where Tom Cousins acquired his concepts, he responded: "I think of what Atlanta might need 20 years from now and build it now."

Another entrepreneur with sky-high vision, Allen G. Paulson became not only a world-famous aviator but also CEO of Gulfstream Aerospace. Allen Paulson and his flight crew captured two world speed records to show the capabilities of his new Gulfstream IV. First he flew westbound from the 1987 Paris airshow and eight months later (beating a record set by a Boeing 747SP), he flew eastbound from Houston. These two flights established or beat 35 international speed and distance records. The records stood until the early 90s, and that record was only toppled by a Concorde jet! These events stirred almost as much excitement as the legendary Charles Lindbergh's around-the-world flight.

Asked what he could possibly envision next, Paulson modestly replied, "Oh, this is old news. We've worked for months on our next design. You keep making advances." As Albert Einstein said:

"IMAGINATION IS MORE IMPORTANT THAN KNOWLEDGE."

What and how a man or woman visualizes today obviously is foundational to where the individual will become one year or ten years from now. Youthful people of any age seem always to be enthralled with a picture of something far beyond their everyday existence. Perhaps a vision starts in a modest or not so modest way, a dictionary or a golf course, but the more detailed and realistic it becomes in a person's mind, the more one asks "Why not?" or "What if?" Thus, that vision becomes more exciting, and the more likely it is that a person may look out her window and see thousands of children with dictionaries in their hands, or a person who loves his city may see his vision grow into hundreds of new jobs within newly prosperous neighborhoods.

When we do the best we can with what we have, visualization becomes easier. When we envision the life we want to lead, when we vividly imagine important components of that life, we usually can have whatever we imagine. As Canadian lacrosse player Ryan Ward said:

> ***"MY VISUALIZATION TAKES PLACE BEFORE, THE DAY BEFORE, ALL DURING THE GAME, AND EVEN INTO THE GAME ITSELF; YOU KNOW, WHAT I WANT TO DO ON THE NEXT PLAY, WHAT I WANT TO DO ON THE NEXT SHIFT. I DEFINITELY USE THAT STRATEGY."***

The more we see, feel, and desire, the more likely it will become manifest. Think of the life you desire to live and the qualities you desire to possess. See the things you desire to accomplish and the person you will become. Visualize the ways you will invest your time, effort, and resources. Think of the talents you possess and the ways you will maximize and use them. Think, think, think, because that is the best and most likely way in which you can become the person you desire to be.

With God's help and your faith, you can become whatever you desire to be. Visualize the qualities you desire to possess: greater compassion, nobler convictions, greater empathy, greater understanding, proven integrity, more courage, or more abundant love. Think of undesirable elements you desire to overcome: greed and selfishness, jealousy, hatred, and lack of forgiveness.

Good attitudes and excellent thinking, visualizing oneself without negative failure traits, builds the strong character each one of us desires. The Holy Bible tells us to overcome evil with good, to love our neighbor as ourselves, to treat others as we would like them to treat us. To implement such thinking, and use our positive emotions to fuel our positive thoughts, we must capture the vision of the life we aspire to live. Doing the best we can with what we have in every aspect of our life, is the surest way to happiness and personal achievement.

The greatest opportunity we have is to create a vision of the life we desire to live and the purpose to live for that will make that life possible.

"VISUALIZATION IS DAYDREAMING WITH A PURPOSE."

—*Bo Bennett*
Author

CHAPTER 10

The Right Attitude

THE ATTITUDE WE project through our voice, words, and mannerisms determines the effect we have on those who come under our sphere of influence.

Merriam Webster defines attitude as "a feeling or way of thinking that affects a person's behavior." The choice of words often suggests an individual's temperament and the qualities of character they possess. We each have our own understanding of spoken words without them being defined. Intuitively, we instantaneously perceive another person's attitude. What follows that perception is up to us to interpret as we will.

Some people are immediately recognized as winners. Invariably such individuals determined at some point in their lives how they would approach each day and each person in a consistent manner. When we do the best we can with what we have, our attitude becomes a dynamic part of our success and substance. Our attitude emerges from our soul and mind and our will and emotions. Most people are sensible, probably most are fair, and most have good will toward others. But it is our emotions which often gain the upper hand in our expressions. In this case, even well-meaning people yield to laziness, excuse-making, angry outbursts, and road rage. We can't always control circumstances, but we can always control our attitude, which helps us master our circumstances. As minister, leadership authority, and author John C. Maxwell said:

"PEOPLE MAY HEAR YOUR WORDS, BUT THEY FEEL YOUR ATTITUDE."

Consider some of the institutions which instill strong attitudes throughout their personnel. The military, airlines, first responders, commercial businesses, and others know that employee attitude means everything in terms of military success, public safety, customer satisfaction, and similar outcomes.

The line grew longer at an airline ticket booth as an irate client demanded answers from a courteous attendant. Midway in the line, a small boy questioned his mother, "Mom, does that man need a timeout?"

As other people stifled their chuckles, the customer looked at the lad, turned to the airline attendant, and said, "I guess I do. I needed that." He apologized and accepted his boarding pass, after being reminded of something every small child should be taught at home: to learn the right and proper attitudes and use them throughout your life. Most who succeed do exactly that.

Military service exemplifies some of the finest training, not just in good attitudes, but in the formation of interpersonal attitudes that create, as they say, "a band of brothers," each protective of the next. Pride, obedience, personal responsibility, courtesy, respect for authority, and similar traits are drilled into each recruit until such attitudes become automatic. These become not just admirable qualities but life-saving attributes. Throughout world history, heroic legends have been made by individuals willing to think and feel, not just for themselves, but for their comrades and beyond.

An unforgettable story from December 22, 1944, concerned a group of enemy soldiers who approached an American outpost, waving white flags. The two officers and two enlisted men had come to offer the Americans an opportunity to surrender. The private first class they approached consulted the staff sergeant, who blindfolded the officers and drove them to Bastogne, Belgium, to take their request to Brigadier General Anthony C. McAuliffe of the 101st Airborne Division.

The Acting Chief of Staff, Lieutenant Colonel Ned Moore, entered General McAuliffe's sleeping quarters, awakened the general, and told him, "The Germans have sent some people forward to take our surrender." Moore recalled that McAuliffe, still half asleep, said "Nuts!"

In a meeting with his staff shortly thereafter, he angrily declared that "Americans have no intention of surrendering," and wondered how to phrase those intentions in a written communique back to the German commander.

"What you said initially would be hard to beat," Lieutenant Colonel Harry Kinnard, his Division Operations Officer said.

McAulliffe asked, "What do you mean?"

Kinnard replied, "Sir, you said 'Nuts.'"

All members of the staff enthusiastically agreed, so McAulliffe wrote it down on a message pad and said, "Have it typed up."

The word "NUTS" was centered in large type on a sheet of paper and returned with the four messengers. That story hit every news outlet in America during one of the most intense times of combat. Morale within the military and home front soared. General McAuliffe's firm attitude transformed minds and spirits approaching a lonely, difficult Christmas season.

Doing all we can with what we have keeps us prepared for whatever may happen. The IT genius wearing mismatched socks was not dressed for success when he prepared to impress his boss's friend, who wanted new ideas for his large corporation. Each of us can tell humorous stories about those whose lack of simple preparedness left them far behind. Ask anyone who has left home without their wallet, driver's license, or cell phone. Without any one of these objects, our attitude becomes severely altered. As former football player and coach Lou Holtz said:

> *"ABILITY IS WHAT YOU'RE CAPABLE OF DOING. MOTIVATION DETERMINES WHAT YOU DO. ATTITUDE DETERMINES HOW WELL YOU DO IT."*

Everyone's attitude begins with the way they feel and act toward themselves. Self-respect is essential. Doing all we can with what we have engenders respect for ourselves and others. Rudeness, indifference, and noncooperation do not result from the other person, but from how we feel about ourselves. Everyone deserves the utmost respect and gratitude for who they are and what they have accomplished.

It helps to question ourselves from time to time as to our attitude about our mind, body, and spirit. Neglect any of these, or fail to take account of powerful and often hidden emotions within ourselves, and our attitudes can make us ineffective, weak, bitter, ungrateful, or angry. Such self-defeating beliefs as "I always do this," "This is not my day," or "I don't see how I can"—even the tone of voice we use toward ourselves—either diminishes or encourages us.

Until we honor the person we are, we are unlikely to honor our parents, spouse, children, neighbors, or anyone else. Each day we should begin with a personal attitude check. Use your mind and thoughts to prepare yourself to make your day into a day of effectiveness and productivity. As one person said, "We have two ways to begin each day: either good morning, God, or good God it's morning." It's our decision to make.

Attitude is an hour-by-hour, lifelong series of decisions. The earlier we decide certain things, the easier it becomes to engage in excellent relationships and accept good opportunities. With all other things equal, the polite and helpful individual is chosen over others. Someone fit and well-dressed exhibits an attitude of good health and energy. A friendly approach often defuses an angry opponent. In a myriad of ways, good attitudinal self-training becomes a major part of doing all you can with what you have.

As we mature and good attitudes strengthen, we discover that gratitude is among the most important attributes we can possess. I know how I feel when someone takes the time to write me a letter of appreciation. A person's gratitude is one of the finest gifts and most influential qualities they can possess.

As I related earlier, the CEO who mentored a visiting trainee and received an orchid from her said, "I started to take that beautiful flower to my wife, but decided it made my office come alive. Her imaginative gift interested me strongly and, as a result, I have followed that young woman's career in our company." That woman's gift showed she appreciated not only her company's CEO and his gift of counsel, but also his office surroundings. Her gratitude told much about her attitude of awareness and respect.

The late Earl Nightingale, the beloved motivational speaker, offered a list of attitudes, entitled "Fifteen Ways to Keep Miserable":

- *Think about yourself.*
- *Talk about yourself.*
- *Use the personal pronoun "I" as often as possible.*
- *Mirror yourself continually in the opinion of others.*
- *Listen greedily to what people say about you.*
- *Insist on consideration and respect.*
- *Demand agreement with your own views on everything.*
- *Sulk if people are not grateful to you for favors shown them.*
- *Never forget a service you may have rendered.*
- *Expect to be appreciated.*
- *Be suspicious.*

- *Be sensitive to slights.*
- *Be jealous and envious of others.*
- *Never forget a criticism.*
- *Trust nobody but yourself.*

Leaders lead by righteous attitudes, as much as any other strength of character. As motivational speaker Brian Tracy said: "Develop an attitude of gratitude, and give thanks for everything that happens to you, knowing that every step forward is a step toward achieving something bigger and better than your current situation."

We all follow those who exhibit strength of character. A great aspect of a positive attitude is the determination to never accept defeat. At any moment plans can become disrupted. Many well-remembered stories illustrate this point, but a favorite concerns England's Prime Minister Winston Churchill. Invited in 1941 to address his old school, Harrow, Churchill said, "Never give in, never give in, never, never, never, never—in nothing, great or small, large or petty—never give in except to convictions of honor and good sense."

> **"NOTHING CAN STOP THE MAN WITH THE RIGHT MENTAL ATTITUDE FROM ACHIEVING HIS GOAL; NOTHING ON EARTH CAN HELP THE MAN WITH THE WRONG MENTAL ATTITUDE."**
>
> —THOMAS JEFFERSON

CHAPTER 11

Think!

THOMAS J. WATSON'S famous slogan, "THINK" was adopted by his IBM Corporation in the 1920s. The slogan has lasted through succeeding decades, past the typewriter era and into the computer technology age. Such devices as the ThinkPad carry the motto forward. Ironically, as more and more of us use the marvelous advances which offer a world of outside information, fewer people actually think for themselves. The information age is powerful, but so is the human mind. Anyone who does the hard work of processing his or her own thoughts about an individual situation learns to respect the process and power within any so-called ordinary mind. The more we learn to think, the more we become willing to think, and the more our specific life purpose emerges. The thinking mind seeks education and valid experience. As Nelson Mandela said:

"EDUCATION IS THE MOST POWERFUL WEAPON WHICH YOU CAN USE TO CHANGE THE WORLD."

By this time, parents, schools, jobs, the military, or any other number of personal factors have given you far more knowledge and experience than you realize. At any point in our adult life, the aggregate of these benefits becomes astounding. As our education and experience increases through the decades, a thoughtful person discovers the most beneficial capacities they possess reside within their mind in the form of their thoughts. As we move into an increasingly meaningful life, many of us see the importance of our daydreams and visions, but few of us allow ourselves specific periods of time for deeper thinking and visualizing the potential we possess.

Thinking, especially concentrated, focused thinking, in place of drifting thoughts and various ideas, is the only way to think productively. If a challenge is complex or frustrating, we often find the solution difficult to comprehend. The real problem solvers that I have known and admired were those who possessed a creative mind and visualized the possibilities of their creative efforts. Mental dynamite is the power contained within the thoughts of dynamic individuals who believe in themselves and their capacity to achieve their objectives. We develop this power of visualization and implementation through our faith in ourselves and in our abilities to achieve our objectives.

Every mature human brain contains a treasure chest of knowledge and experience. As Eleanor Roosevelt said:

"PEOPLE GROW THROUGH EXPERIENCE IF THEY MEET LIFE HONESTLY AND COURAGEOUSLY. THIS IS HOW CHARACTER IS BUILT."

The cognitive part of the human brain—the CEO that directs our thinking—consists of only 5 percent, with the remaining 95 percent reserved for the power of wisdom contained in our subconscious or spiritual mind. This superior, all-encompassing mind is the reservoir of worldly wisdom containing all that has been learned, felt, or experienced. The thinking part of our brain continually draws from our creative source of wisdom. Our subconscious habits and impressions form the primary structure of most people's lives, but those who consciously discipline themselves and direct their thinking to creative thoughts, merge their conscious mind and its thoughts with their subconscious mind and its creative capacities. In other words, our past successes lend substance to our visions, joining the present to the future, and our experience to the fulfillment of our aspirations.

Try using your thinking power to recall your past successes and help you more fully understand the possibilities that are within your grasp. Perhaps it was an award or promotion, or maybe a hole-in-one on the golf course. Remember the pleasure, the excitement, and the feelings of gratitude and achievement. Add that picture of success to the one your present thoughts are projecting and visualize the outcome your experience and ability will make possible. Too often people believe they are thinking when they are listing the obstacles that stand in the way of their success. They look not at their objective but instead visualize circumstances, doubts, and potential problems. Focus your mind on your worthy objectives, not on the myriad difficulties which could prevent them. What we focus our thoughts on we increase. We all know people who focus their thoughts on difficult circumstances and argue that there is no way out. They are right. When you use your mind and thoughts wisely, virtually any goal within reason can be accomplished.

Perhaps you, like me, feel your education has been severely limited. Today, more than at any other time in the past, individuals who lack a college degree believe they cannot achieve a future comparable to someone who earns one or more degrees. Among the countless arguments to that idea, I could name a mayor of a large city, an entrepreneurial multimillionaire, and a little nun who changed the face of modern charity and recently was elevated to sainthood by the Roman Catholic Church. Academic achievement certainly is highly desirable and worth striving for, but lack of such educational benefits should never preclude worthwhile achievements.

Today men and women in the workforce operate within an overwhelmingly information-based society. The challenge is to stay up-to-date with career demands. Those who choose to continually learn, who focus on their future needs and outlooks, find numerous ways to acquire further education. People as old as 90 obtain college degrees. It is no longer unusual to see a grandparent and grandchild receive their diplomas at the same ceremony.

Learning is a living experience and our life increases as we increase in knowledge and experience. This is not merely academic, of course, but equally performance-based. There's an old joke about someone who asked a New Yorker, "How do I get to Carnegie Hall?" "Practice, practice, practice," was the response. As Benjamin Franklin said:

"AN INVESTMENT IN KNOWLEDGE PAYS THE BEST INTEREST."

If you will set a learning goal for each year of your life, you will be amazed by the value of the wisdom you will gain! If you will increase the use of your mind through positive, creative thinking at that same rate, you can change your life in keeping with your highest desires and greatest aspirations. "To know what you know and what you do not know, that is true knowledge," said Confucius. Our best future consists of filling our mind with the finest thoughts we are capable of thinking.

Our gratitude for all we have been privileged to learn and experience makes us eager to expand our knowledge further. A group of professional women held a monthly luncheon meeting wherein each member was expected to announce a recent personal or professional victory.

"A promotion," "A new client," "A newspaper feature article," and so forth, seemed like a roomful of high achievement until, at last, an obviously intimidated newcomer said in a small voice, "I paid the rent." Cheers erupted as the young woman received a standing ovation. Everyone in the room understood the statement. To pay the rent, to keep on keeping on, often can be as fine a learning experience as any other. The so-called "school of hard knocks" has much to teach us, but most of us are glad to graduate. The quality and substance of our finest thoughts can speed up the process of our education and self-development far more than most people realize.

Adversity often cannot be helped. Sometimes a combination of unusual circumstances leaves a family or individual needing to "Look up in order to touch bottom." That's when our faith and the best use of our talents proves the most advantageous. During the Great Depression, many suicides occurred because of business failures and many people were forced to declare bankruptcy. In those days, bankruptcy was considered morally unthinkable. I know what it meant, because it was then that my father lost his fortune, his partner, and his health.

Johnny Mercer, the great American songwriter, purportedly paid the last of his father's business debts of $300,000 and restored the family's honor with proceeds from an immensely popular song with the catchy title, *Ac-Cent-Tchu-Ate the Positive*. The thought in his verse—"accentuate the positive, eliminate the negative, latch on to the affirmative, don't mess with mister in between"—may seem simplistic when a situation appears desperate, but the formula is excellent.

When we do all we can with what we have, we invariably find that we have within ourselves most of what we need. Beyond that, some of the most comforting words in the Holy Bible are: "It came to pass..." Looking at a distressing period of any life can seem daunting, but the fact is that most problems are temporary and not necessarily permanent.

The program advocated here results not in self-actualization, but should become a means of projecting one's life into new confidence, stability, and imaginative thinking. An atmosphere of order and purpose engenders more brilliant ideas than most of us realize can be produced. Two stories that I know about illustrate this point.

A career criminal had approached age 40 before his life changed radically. Since adolescence, the largely uneducated man had committed petty crimes, which kept him in and out of prisons well into the years that he should have been productive. His prison behavior was usually troublesome, since a hot temper and rebellious spirit were his trademarks. Eventually he was rewarded with another assignment to solitary confinement for the longest stretch yet. It didn't bother him, as he always emerged with his usual bad attitudes. This time, however, he picked up the only book in his cell, the Holy Bible, opened it at random, and found his eyes resting on a single sentence: "…be ye transformed by the renewing of your mind." He closed the book; he was not interested.

In the days that followed, curious questions began to form in his thinking: "How many days, months, and years had he occupied prison cells during his lifetime?" As he pondered this thought, other questions formed: "Exactly how much had he stolen during those years and approximately how much money had he acquired?" Another time he asked himself: "How much per hour had he probably acquired over the years he hustled other peoples' money and goods?" He had no pencil and paper, but plenty of time to consider the answers. At length, he decided he had earned possibly eleven cents an hour during his life up to that time.

When he picked up the Bible again and opened it, he immediately read a passage that changed his life: "If any man be in Christ, he is a new creature; old things have passed away and all things are new." If that were true, the man reasoned, perhaps he should explore the idea. Another kind of life seemed impossible, but he began to read and to wonder.

Success, Substance, and Significance

Jailers found a new man when this prisoner was released from solitary confinement, but this is not unusual. Jailhouse conversions are commonplace, they said. When our friend was released into society, he was ready to attempt to change his attitude and actions. He decided to try to find every home and business he had robbed over the years. He would confess the crime, ask for forgiveness, and promise to attempt restitution. The effort took some time and he did not remember every house or office he had burglarized, but as he approached his victims sincerely, he discovered to his disbelief that all but one forgave him.

The visit he most dreaded was a chain grocery store he robbed several years earlier. He waited for the manager to appear and saw a formidable-looking individual approach. The manager had little time, seemed unfriendly, and asked what our friend wanted. Haltingly, the former convict confessed details of his misdeed. The manager nodded his head, remembering.

"Do you have a job?" he asked. "How can you repay us?"

There was no job for an uneducated, untrained fellow who knew little beyond thievery and incarceration. He stood there, humiliated.

"You can work here, starting in the stockroom," the manager offered. "If you mean what you say, we'll help you until you can find something better."

The man's mind indeed had been renewed. He gratefully accepted an entry-level job and worked faithfully at various duties until he became an assistant manager. He was extremely loyal to the man who hired him and the place where he worked, and has remained there for many years. In addition, he reaches out to others like himself and helps them reintegrate into society. His story is dramatic proof that any mind can be transformed at any stage of life.

In 1974, Mr. Richard Montañez was working as a janitor at the Frito Lay factory in Southern California. "Nobody noticed me," he told a network television audience. "I just showed up and did my work." At this point in his story, Mr. Montañez stressed the importance of his wife's role in what happened next. "She prayed every day for God to give me a revelation, and I prayed the same prayer. I did my job and we continued to pray. One day, a single word seemed to come from nowhere: 'Chili.'" The word surprised him and he pondered it. What had chili to do with anything? Possibly the connection happened when he opened his favorite snack food, Cheetos. He instantly realized that spicy chili powder added to Cheetos would be an instantaneous hit with fellow Hispanics. His wife agreed.

Next came the problem of how a janitor could augment his corporation's products. After more prayer, Mr. Montañez decided to telephone the corporation's CEO, headquartered in another city. He finally reached the CEO's assistant, who seemed not too helpful, but asked what his position was in the company. Intrigued by the fact that a janitor was telephoning with an idea, she put the call through to their chief executive.

After hearing Mr. Montañez's suggestion, the CEO said, "I will come to your plant within two weeks. Have a marketing plan ready, and I'll look at it."

That day Mr. Montañez faced his next big hurdle. "I'm in trouble," he told his wife. "What is a marketing plan?" She didn't know, but suggested they go to the library and find a book about marketing plans. "For the next two weeks, she and I studied chapters one through five," he recalled. "We went over and over the information, until we could put together a plan for me to present."

Meanwhile, word from the CEO to his factory manager had filtered through various vice presidents and division heads throughout the factory. There were questions about a janitor presenting a marketing plan to a corporate CEO. The day before the meeting, Mr. Montañez paid $3.50 for a necktie and had someone teach him how to tie it. On the big day, he arrived nervous but prepared to do his best. To his great surprise, he found himself well able to articulate his ideas before the company leaders.

Everything went well until someone in the marketing department asked a question: "What market share do you anticipate?"

He was dumbfounded by the question and unable to answer. "We only went through Chapter 5," he recalled humorously. He simply spread two fingers wide against a displayed pie chart. He had no idea about what he was doing.

"We'll do it," the corporation's chief decided. That was the birthday of Flamin' Hot Cheetos. That also began a career journey for Mr. Montañez. It has involved much on-the-job business training, leading to significant influence and business decisions concerning tastes and desires of those in his culture. He is now the executive vice president of multicultural sales and community activation for PepsiCo North America.

If his story seems almost impossible, I'll say Mr. Montañez would not agree. A humble man with strong convictions, Richard Montañez inspires fellow Americans of every background to seek God for their specific calling. With God's help, any mind created can learn, prosper, and achieve unlimited good for countless others.

As we do what we can with what we have, we discover that a mind thoughtfully and faithfully utilized, increases exponentially in wisdom and power. Translate that idea into increased mind power and you can visualize the limitless potential you possess in the way your thoughts influence your life.

> **KNOWLEDGE IS POWER. INFORMATION IS LIBERATING. EDUCATION IS THE PREMISE OF PROGRESS IN EVERY SOCIETY, IN EVERY FAMILY.**
>
> — *KOFI ANNAN*
> 7TH SECRETARY GENERAL, UN

CHAPTER 12

Expectations and Opportunities

"We will always tend to fulfill our own expectation of ourselves," said motivational speaker Brian Tracy. When we do all we can with what we have, our self-expectations increase as we experience the results of our efforts and achievements. At times we may feel inhibited or unable to move forward, with little hope of achieving our objectives, but by doing our best on a daily basis, we invariably increase our confidence and determination to do what we are capable of doing. Every time we succeed at anything, we increase our confidence in our ability. As Rosabeth Moss Kanter, a professor of business at Harvard Business School, said:

"CONFIDENCE ISN'T OPTIMISM OR PESSIMISM, AND IT'S NOT A CHARACTER ATTRIBUTE. IT'S THE EXPECTATION OF A POSITIVE OUTCOME."

Doing all that we can with what we have requires energy and energy begets greater energy. The force of positive, creative energy stimulates our expectations and increases our commitment to achieve the objectives we establish. We must learn to appreciate the capacities we possess. When we have the proper attitude and motivation, we recognize the greatness of our capacities. Our competent expectations can become a tremendous attribute when focused on worthy causes. I have seen miracles take place when a group of capable community leaders were inspired by a worthy objective. Most of us who succeed have witnessed the power and influence of noble objectives. Intuitively, we each desire to be part of something noble, something that is worthy of the best within us. It is the greatness of worthy objectives that inspires us to do the best we can with what we have.

Expect each day to offer a new beginning, even if each day may seem the same as the day before. Doing all we can do with what we have revitalizes our efforts and expands our creativity. We learn to do things better with shortcuts, new methods, and time-saving procedures. We discover more of our innovative and creative thoughts as we expect greater results from our efforts. Lack of progress, even in the most mundane tasks, leads to stagnation and defeat. We must continually move forward if we hope to expand our capacities. We can never stand still because that is moving backward.

A man who could not write a coherent business letter found numerous ways to have his secretary write a "first draft." The day she quit her job, he realized he needed to learn how to write a simple business letter. Reviewing some of hers and buying a book about letter writing helped the businessman build a file of sample letters, which he used with variations from that time forward. By doing his best, he became capable of writing excellent business letters that produced positive and profitable results.

If indeed, as Benjamin Franklin said, "Necessity is the mother of invention," many people resist the need to invent. They struggle to maintain a status quo—hiding their weaknesses and attempting to cover their failures—and thus keep themselves from expecting much more than they presently possess. Thomas Edison said:

"OPPORTUNITY IS MISSED BY MOST PEOPLE BECAUSE IT IS DRESSED IN OVERALLS AND LOOKS LIKE WORK."

As the businessman above discovered, it took very little extra work to learn how to handle his correspondence, compared to the years of effort it took to avoid it. His self-expectation rose and his confidence grew as he began to express his ideas clearly and forcefully, and in addition learned to speak more fluently and effectively. By doing his best he became far more successful than he imagined he could.

The more we commit ourselves to doing our best, the more we increase our ability to produce and achieve greater results in less time with less effort. The individual committed to excellence sets an example that makes him stand out among others. When a job must be done right the first time, when strict accuracy is required, and truth that passes all legal standards, this is the time we must do our best. Is that expecting too much? Not for the person who desires to live his life beyond the ordinary. It is by going the extra mile, doing more than is expected, giving greater effort, and doing finer work that makes the difference between the average and the exceptional!

During my early life on our Minnesota farm, my parents discovered that I had a talent for communication in written and spoken form. They encouraged me to develop this talent and fill my mind with positive thoughts. They also encouraged me to look upon the many difficult problems we faced as opportunities that contained possibilities. When our food was limited, my mother focused on how good it tasted. When it rained, my father spoke of how much the crops would benefit. When we were snowed in, we spoke of how fortunate we were to have wood to burn. The less we had the more we appreciated what we had. It was always gratitude in place of despair, always hope in place of fear.

Gradually I began to understand the potential that could reside within me if I would do the best I could with what I had. I began to focus my thoughts and words on everything positive, and to see the best in every situation we faced and every person I met. In doing this, everything seemed better than it was before. Even though nothing had changed, it just seemed better.

By encouraging me to change my thinking, my parents helped me see new opportunities and possibilities. These did not come about immediately, but they were there when I needed them. New expectations created new opportunity for me to develop my mind and thoughts in preparation for what was to come. A popular American writer, Orison Swett Marden, wrote:

"THERE IS NO MEDICINE LIKE HOPE, NO INCENTIVE SO GREAT, AND NO TONIC SO POWERFUL AS EXPECTATION OF SOMETHING TOMORROW."

It was that something good that inspired me to believe in the possibilities the future would hold for me, if I would do my best with what I had.

Doing all we can with what we have involves hard work. On the abandoned farm that my father bought when I was 12, I became the main source of labor as I left my boyhood behind and became a working man. My father was too ill to do heavy work and my mother devoted herself to the care of her beloved husband with serious health problems and a growing boy who both parents loved. Daily my father instructed me on my work schedule, dictating my duties but never telling me how to perform them. The goal was always beyond my grasp and my workday lasted from early morning until late at night. I knew how much my help was needed and respected my father too much to offer objections, but at times I wondered why he expected so much from me. It almost seemed like a living hell as I grew older and my work became more intensive and more demanding.

However, as I gradually developed, I began to understand some of the reasons he was so demanding. He wanted me to become a man worthy of manhood and willing to do my best at whatever I did. When I plowed the fields, planted the crops, and tended them until harvest time, I was proud of the harvest when it was reaped, as I saw the results of my constant efforts. I did my best to set straight fences, plow straight furrows, and do the best I could at whatever I did. I learned how to be satisfied with my honest efforts. My father demanded my best efforts always. If it wasn't my best, it wasn't worthy of my effort. My father's demands were challenging and far more important than I realized at the time. He insisted that what I did was the best I could do, and if it wasn't, I had to do it over again. I soon saw the difference as the seeded crop came out of the ground. Because of his training, no one ever needed to remind me to do it right the first time.

Blessed are those who learn early in life the importance of each aspect of their mind, will, thoughts, and emotions. When our mind defines what is best, and we summon the will to do what we know is best, we will receive greater satisfaction from the challenges we face. The desire for excellence exists in each of us, whether we realize it or not. The achievement of our best efforts transforms our life and makes us into the person we are capable of being. Nothing worthwhile ever happens without dedicated, concentrated effort.

You might wonder, as I did, how those many acres of perfectly straight rows of corn could lead a youth on the path of high expectation and future opportunity. It seems unlikely, but even at that age, I understood and respected the fact that my parents wanted to sow the best seeds of knowledge and ethical behavior into my mind. There could be no finer heritage and I have lived long enough to understand how few of us are so privileged to have parents willing to help us become the best person we are capable of being.

Each man, woman, and child on earth can use their mind, will, and emotions to teach themselves the desirable traits and habits that will improve their lives. We can aspire to learn, and do, and become more than we see in ourselves today. Truth, humility, understanding, and compassion for ourselves and our families will strengthen our hopes and help make us into the person God intended for us to be.

Self-help methods employed to further our personal development will often work for a time. We all know those so-called "self-made men," but such individuals rarely have much lasting influence beyond their own small perimeter. The individual who desires to use each day as a stepping stone towards a divinely designed destiny, is motivated to think beyond themselves for a greater, more lasting purpose. Rewards for good efforts always come, but not necessarily in the form we imagine or at the time we expect.

My father lost his fortune, his partner, and his health during the Great Depression of 1929 to 1934, when he was one of the leading businessmen in Hollywood. For reasons I will never know we moved from our California home to that abandoned farm in Northern Minnesota. In 1955, after a dozen years of hard work and steady improvement, our registered herd of dairy cattle fell prey to a serious disease and we lost all we had worked so hard to achieve. I was required to leave the farm to find work to support my parents and establish a profession. At a time of such heartbreak, my parents remained resolute. Eventually, because of the seeds of hope and character they had planted in my mind, I found work, we were able to regain a good life, and move into greater opportunities, living far beyond our hopes and expectations. Henry Ford addressed such situations saying:

"FAILURE IS SIMPLY THE OPPORTUNITY TO BEGIN AGAIN, THIS TIME MORE INTELLIGENTLY."

Doing all we can with what we have may seem a repetition of thought and admonition, but change happens gradually as our perception changes in positive and productive ways. When we do things by rote and vain repetition, change cannot occur, but as we attempt to make things better, change happens in wonderful ways. As the inventor, engineer, and businessman Charles Kettering said, "High achievement always takes place in the framework of high expectation." When we expect more of ourselves, we are seldom disappointed.

As someone once said, "If you want to achieve greatness, stop asking for permission." From your position of doing all you can with what you have, you will initiate new opportunity. Doing things well with what we have makes us appreciate who we are and what we have achieved. Thus, our thoughts travel with new expectations and greater aspirations. With a little creative initiative and a vision of what is possible, our ideas can achieve surprising success. Housewives have turned cookies, pickles, jams, pies, frozen biscuits, and even pimento cheese into multimillion-dollar success stories.

Grace Kinsler, a Knoxville housewife and mother of two daughters, was a devout woman who listened regularly to a California religious radio program. She felt strongly that she wanted to send money to help support this ministry and asked her husband if they could donate. He replied they were giving well beyond their tithe and he felt they could not give more. Grace wondered what she could do to find money for her cause. She said "I wasn't an exceptional cook, but everyone always complimented me on my pimento cheese. I asked the corner grocer if he would sell it and he agreed."

The cheese spread sold so readily that stores asked for other items they could sell under Mrs. Kinsler's label. In time, she had factories in 38 states and products in most of the nation's chain grocery stores. The devout woman not only surpassed her most vivid imaginings, but enjoyed passing along much of her prosperity to those who taught and worked for the less fortunate.

Mrs. Kinsler, like the enormously successful Mrs. Debbi Fields, who turned homemade cookies into a mega-success, began by doing all they could with what they had. Each turned ordinary ingredients found in almost any kitchen into extraordinary ideas rich with profits for many and customer pleasure for millions.

I can relate to Grace Kinsler's story about her early life and her father's teaching about growing lettuce. She helped him prepare soil for the lettuce beds, explaining that lettuce seeds are so tiny that the beds must be extra-carefully prepared. She recalled sifting soil through many screenings until it was "fine as silk." As she worked side-by-side with her father, watching his careful preparation and eventually his pleasure as delicate seedlings emerged, Grace said those experiences made her realize very early the importance of every day's careful, thorough activities.

In just that way, as we do all we can with what we have, we can confidently expect our work, our thoughts, and our attitudes to produce good crops. These successes come forth in multiple ways, but the intangible often proves more substantial than anything we see or hold in our hands. One benefit is confidence, for as we do all we can each day, confident expectations invariably arise. As our mind, our hands, and our heart combine more effectively, we learn to feel confident about our life as others place their confidence in us. Such benefits can't be measured on any scale, but they are real and lasting if we appreciate what we have and what we achieve.

These efforts create one of the most priceless benefits of all—that of a good conscience and wholesome satisfaction. Our good work, especially when it involves the participation and benefit to others, is the outward manifestation of our character and sincerity, and the embodiment of the truths for which we stand.

Appreciating what we possess today, no matter how little or how much we possess, creates a form of gratitude that rejects what most people consider ordinary because of its simplicity and sincerity. I think often of a story I heard long ago about a man who met a band of thieves who robbed him. You would not expect that event to produce gratitude, but this was his summation:

> *"1. I was never robbed before.*
> *"2. They took my purse but not my life.*
> *"3. My purse contained my all, but it was very little.*
> *"4. I am grateful I was robbed and not the robber."*

When we do all we can with what we have, whatever we have within ourselves is enough to fulfill our present needs. By knowing we are equal to our needs, this leads to the confidence that we are worthy of being trusted with more.

What if we expect more, yet for months or years see no opportunity? Many, including myself, have experienced long periods of drudgery and hardship, with repetitive, purposeless duties that seemed to lead nowhere. At such times as these, it is tempting to imagine that there is nothing beyond what we see, but that is never true. The scriptures tell us to not be weary in well-doing because in due season we will reap our harvest. The decision to keep on keeping on, as some express it, can either weary us or build us. That is our decision and that is our choice. There always are, and always will be, opportunities for those who desire and seek them. Opportunity arrives at some point in every life, but often the individual is not prepared to accept or receive it.

Mr. and Mrs. Richard Montañez were seeking opportunity and praying for it when his idea arrived. He seized upon it and the outcome has been described as a "Cinderella" story, but it was not that simple. To rise from a janitor's job to that of vice president in a major corporation inevitably required his willingness to study, to learn, and to use his own initiative and ambition to move him from level to level.

Everything about a good life requires our participation. As we do all we can with what we have, even the lowest-level position can be transformed into one of great influence. As those around us feel confident in trusting our values, opportunity appears. Some activists seek opportunities and reject them, always seeking something better, while others accept the first thing that comes along and later regret it. The individuals who know themselves, their talents, and abilities, learn to concentrate their efforts and are not swayed by suggestions or opportunities that fail to meet their major objectives.

Doing all we can to the best of our ability will often lead us to our life's purpose and destiny. Milton Berle once quipped, "If opportunity doesn't knock, build a door." There's some truth in that, but it's also true that those who do all they can with what they have invariably can expect the right opportunity to appear at the right time and feel confident they will know it when it arrives.

Someone has said that no man steps into the same river twice, because he is not the same man and it's not the same river. When we think we're standing still, and our circumstances and duties never seem to change, that is not true. We are changing for the better because our mind is directing our thoughts, hopes, desires, and even our simplest actions. We may not see these subtle changes, but beneath our feet the earth is ever-so-slightly rising.

> *"WITHOUT CHANGE THERE IS NO INNOVATION, CREATIVITY, OR INCENTIVE FOR IMPROVEMENT. THOSE WHO INITIATE CHANGE WILL HAVE A BETTER OPPORTUNITY TO MANAGE THE CHANGE THAT IS INEVITABLE."*
>
> — WILLIAM POLLARD
> PHYSICIST AND AUTHOR

Part Three: Where You Are

"Happiness doesn't start when this, that, or the other thing is resolved. Happiness is what happens now when you appreciate what you have."

SENORA ROY

CHAPTER 13

Where You Are

PRESIDENT THEODORE ROOSEVELT said: "In any moment of decision, the best thing you can do is the right thing, the next best thing is the wrong thing, and the worst thing you can do is nothing." Your life at this moment reflects multiple decisions you have made in the past, which strongly affect where you are today. When my father taught me to do the best I could with what I had where I was, I was too young to realize that where I was at that time was the foundation of my destiny. We were living in an abandoned farm house on an abandoned farm. When a person learns how to live without electricity or a telephone, without natural gas or running water, and to heat and cook with wood, they learn how to make decisions and rely on those they make. My father's strong decision making would, in little more than a dozen years, take us from an abandoned, unproductive farm with nothing but weeds and thistles, to a productive and producing farm with registered dairy cattle and outstanding crops. The abandoned farm on which we lived became the Triple J Stock Farm, one of the finest and most productive farms in Cass County, Minnesota.

I am sure that my father and mother, as well as myself, often wondered why we were there, but the subject was never addressed in my presence. My father had undergone a nervous breakdown because of his business losses during the Great Depression and the death of his beloved partner. In addition, he was ill with a chronic disease. At that time, I was in my early teens, and doing a man's work seven days a week, with responsibilities far beyond my ability to manage. It was at that time that I asked my beloved mother the penetrating question: "Why must we struggle as we do on this farm and what is the purpose for the life I am living?"

My mother must have anticipated I would one day ask that question, when she answered, "Jackie, I think you should ask your heavenly Father for the answer you are seeking."

From that day forward, I continually prayed, "Dear Father, help me find the purpose for my life." As the years passed, my work continued to increase. I saw things gradually changing for the better because of our dedicated efforts and my father's careful planning. But I could not see, at that time, that where I was would prepare me for where I was destined to go. Also at that age, I failed to understand the reason that my father insisted that I learn to do each job well, no matter how difficult it was, as it would be preparing me for the major decisions I would be called upon to make, with the confidence that God was guiding my efforts and decisions. As businessman, author, and philanthropist Tony Robbins said:

"IT IS IN YOUR MOMENTS OF DECISION THAT YOUR DESTINY IS SHAPED."

Where we are at this moment may not require momentous decision, but some of the decisions we make today will affect tomorrow and ultimately generations to come. Everything we have was made possible by someone else. Each person that has lived has made some form of contribution, good or bad, creative or destructive, positive or negative—all have had some form of influence. Those who find it difficult to make decisions that require activation usually delay because of fear or procrastination. Many see their opportunities evaporate because they do not make decisive decisions, so they stay where they are and live with regret. We can and must "decide to decide" if we are to fulfill our purpose and our destiny.

Plato said it well: "A good decision is based on knowledge and not on numbers."

Here are seven mental and spiritual concepts by which I choose to guide my life:

1. *An undoubting and unquestioning faith.*
2. *A simple, direct request for guidance.*
3. *A relaxed and receptive mind.*
4. *A patient and positive awareness.*
5. *An honest self-evaluation.*
6. *Setting no time limit.*
7. *Doing our best at all times.*

An Undoubting and Unquestioning Faith:

God deals with each of us individually. Your faith in His wisdom about your life allows Him to show you His purpose for your life. My Creator's knowledge about every aspect of my life is far more valuable than hundreds of other opinions. Your faith will enable you to work effectively and productively. Your faith will free you from doubt, become the spiritual force that will bring a new power into your life, and open your mind to the possibilities of your potential. Prayer offered with a sense of doubt will be unanswered. Without a strong faith, you will be unable to believe in yourself or in your ability to achieve that for which you pray. Your faith will always be your greatest source of strength.

A Simple and Direct Request for Guidance:

The request you make concerning your purpose is the most important request you will make, because it relates to the fundamental reason for your life. Because of its importance it should be a "prayer offered in faith" with an open mind and the awareness that your faith will bring forth the answer you seek.

A Relaxed and Receptive Mind:

Our faith is the spiritual soil in which our request for guidance is planted. Our request becomes the seed of our planted prayer. Every seed that is planted requires time to develop and grow. The time required for our seed of purpose to grow is determined by the potentials we possess and the magnitude of the purpose we are to fulfill. Our continued prayer, offered in faith, nurtures the seed of our purpose and influences the thoughts and actions that become the purpose for which we have prayed. The preparation for the purpose we are to fulfill requires time, experience, decisions, determination, and dedication. The person who begins as an accountant may move from that profession to others until he or she becomes a banker. We may begin as a teacher and progress to a scientist. We may begin as a builder and later become a minister. What we're doing where we are is leading toward the purpose we are to fulfill.

A Patient and Positive Awareness:

Impatience becomes a destructive influence as we seek to discover our purpose. Impatience causes us to question the answering of our prayer. Time often causes doubt and uncertainty. We diminish our creative abilities when we doubt the receipt of our request. When we assume the responsibility for determining our own fate, in place of allowing God to guide our steps, we nullify our prayer. We must acknowledge our limitations and the fact we are a single entity in the vast world in which we live. Alone we are incapable of visualizing our own potential, but with God's help, all things are possible. Alone we cannot comprehend the power of our mind, or how it relates to the universal mind of our Creator. The possibilities within our purpose are limitless. The scope of our life's mission is beyond our comprehension. It is the will of God within us that dwells within our purpose.

An Honest Self-Evaluation:

As you think of who you are and what you will become, consider your temperament, talents, inclinations, aspirations, values, desires, and expectations. Are you materialistic or altruistic? Are you driven or passive? Are you competitive or conciliatory? Are you a leader or a follower? Are you motivated by a challenge or incentive? Are you spiritual or pragmatic in your thinking? As you answer these questions, you will bring into focus a sense of who you are in relation to your environment. Such understanding will enhance your emotional and intellectual self-perceptions. This focus is needed so you can relate your desires and expectations to those things important to your purpose and happiness. Your unique life's purpose will lead to the fulfillment of your destiny.

Setting no Time Limit:

This decision may be the most difficult part of finding your purpose. We naturally tend to be anxious for something we greatly desire. When we ask a question we want an answer, and when we pray, we desire the answer in the very near future. In seeking guidance, we need direction. Nature itself is often a remarkable teacher, because nature is under the control of the same Power that governs our destiny. There are seasons in nature: a time to plant, a time to nurture, a time to grow, and a time to harvest. There are seasons in human life as we grow from who we are into who we become. Each season has its own time and tasks, its own growing and becoming. In due season you will harvest the opportunities your purpose makes possible – Be Patient.

Doing Our Best Always:
Doing all we can, with what we have, where we are is the ultimate way to develop our talents and abilities. These are the tools we use to fulfill our life's purpose. When we begin to understand our capacity, we have a criterion by which to judge the possibilities within our purpose. Doing all we can where we are creates the opportunity to continually improve what we've done before. The constant improvement of what we do leads us closer to perfection.

By developing the habit of doing all we can, with what we have, where we are, we gain confidence in our ability to handle life's inevitable periods of hardship, disappointment, or loss. Bernie Marcus and Arthur Blank were fired from their executive jobs on the same day in 1978. In a Los Angeles coffee shop, the two men, both avid do-it-yourselfers, formed a vision of a new home improvement business. They imagined an enormous warehouse filled with every item needed for building and home improvement projects. They also wanted a knowledgeable staff of customer service experts.

In 1979, they opened their first two Home Depot mega-stores in Atlanta, Georgia, and a new industry was born. Not only did the Home Depot success become legendary in America's business world, but its influence on home improvement, property management, and individual industry cannot be measured. Millions of homes have added value as dad or even mom refinished floors, added a patio, or learned how to paint. Within 25 years, their company expanded from two stores to 1,700 stores, employing over 300,000 people.

As Arthur Blank said, "Bernie and I founded the Home Depot with a special vision—to create a company that would keep alive the values that were important to us, values like respect among all people, excellent customer service, and giving back to communities and society."

Some executives fired from a position retreat, whereas others, confident in what they have decided, use their firing as a springboard to what they believe they can achieve. Attorney, lawyer, and religious leader James E. Faust said it best:

"SOME OF OUR IMPORTANT CHOICES HAVE A TIME LINE. IF WE DELAY A DECISION, THE OPPORTUNITY IS GONE FOREVER. SOMETIMES OUR DOUBTS KEEP US FROM MAKING A CHOICE THAT INVOLVES CHANGE. THUS AN OPPORTUNITY MAY BE MISSED."

Where we are now will influence whatever happens today or tomorrow. Obviously, the decisions we make today will affect not only today but future days to come. Two unemployed men visualizing a new business model did not imagine they would eventually be employing hundreds of thousands of skilled workers. One argument for doing all we can, with what we have, where we are is that we are as ready as we can be for whatever develops next. Sometimes an opportunity we never dreamed of appears before us. Are we prepared? At other times, some unexpected delay, mishap, or bad circumstance occurs. We need to be as prepared and resourceful as possible.

In adopting this life plan, and seeking guidance from our Creator, we look beyond our limitations to the spiritual power that guides our life. Mr. Montañez prayed for guidance; the word "chili" appeared in his mind, and he followed through. As a janitor, he could not possibly have imagined becoming vice president of a major corporation. Cinderella stories seem to happen to men and women who realize that today is the seedbed for tomorrow's great harvest. They respect each small task or seed within today and learn to put their hearts into whatever they do. A life like this engenders faith in oneself, one's family, friends, and community. This is where we live and move and enjoy our lives to the fullest, meanwhile influencing those around us as we do the best we can with what we have.

Whatever we put our hand to should prosper. Doing all we can at home means family relations and marriages do not fail. We do our best to overcome personal difficulties or discontent whenever frictions arise. We also look at our household in general, maintaining and improving whatever we own. An old car one wishes to replace can be kept clean, shining, and respectable looking. When new things do not immediately appear, or we see no way to obtain them, doing all we can where we are now is a sure way to obtaining what we desire.

No matter who you are or where you are, you will influence more people than you realize. Few of us are conscious of the influence we have on others, yet this influence reaches from generation to generation, from teacher to student, from employer to employee, in an endless chain of small and large events which make up our life. Just as the human body contains more than a trillion individual cells, each human being affects more lives than he or she can possibly count. When we keep our personal influence in mind, we realize our Creator has placed us where He wants us to be, at a time and place He desires us to occupy. Where we are today becomes the entrance to further discovery of the purpose for which we were born. There could be no greater adventure in our life than the arrival of our destiny. The everlasting NOW is the time in which we live, the time of our being, the time of our becoming, the time in which we fulfill our purpose and achieve our potential.

> *"PEOPLE GROW THROUGH EXPERIENCE IF THEY MEET LIFE HONESTLY AND COURAGEOUSLY. THIS IS HOW CHARACTER IS BUILT."*
>
> — Eleanor Roosevelt

CHAPTER 14

What We Believe

OUR THOUGHTS CONTROL our life and what we believe determines what we achieve. If we believe a bright future lies before us, we will envision that future and walk the path that leads to it. If we believe our past mistakes, losses, and bad luck will hinder us, we will believe there is no way for us to go forward to what we desire most. The fact is good things can come from bad circumstances and often do—when we have the right attitude.

Consider Arthur Blank and Bernie Marcus, the two men mentioned in the previous chapter who were fired from their jobs, but envisioned the best home improvement company anyone could possibly develop. Not only did they look beyond the present with their vision, but they obtained the financing needed to open the doors of a business that reflected their viewpoint, and enabled them to encourage hundreds of thousands of individuals to have a more successful and meaningful life. These two outstanding leaders not only dreamed a magnificent dream but saw that dream to completion in a spectacular and productive way.

The Home Depot Corporation not only led in hiring knowledgeable retirees, willing to assist novice customers, but they also featured workshops to teach the public painting, flooring, lawn care, and other similar projects. The community-minded corporation has donated millions of dollars' worth of material assistance to areas affected by natural disasters. This is only one story of two men who needed meaningful work, developed a solution which met their personal needs and beliefs, and changed the lives of untold millions by giving them a greater sense of purpose.

James B. Miller, Jr., a longtime friend, has a similar story about his purposeful business vision. Jim is Chairman of Fidelity Southern Corporation, in charge of numerous banks in Georgia and Florida, with 1,400 employees. As a former practicing attorney, Jim Miller well understood the important role banking institutions play in the life of an individual, family, or corporation. His ideal bank would offer the utmost in personal attention to each customer. Let him tell his story in his own words:

"When I bought the bank in 1976, I was determined to create a bank for the long pull, not for short-term gains, as so many of the start-up banks were focusing on doing here in Georgia. Although we wanted to, and have, made money for our investors, our belief was that if you provided good service at a reasonable price and treated everyone as you wanted to be treated, profits would follow. Fortunately, the original Board of Directors had the same concept I had before I came on the scene.

"Obviously I am an entrepreneurial person and enjoy seeing what I have created and shaped for the future. That is one reason I chose to give up law and build a company which I could touch. I intended to surround myself, and successfully surrounded myself, with people who share that vision and are comfortable being servants to others. We always preach the Golden Rule to all of our new employees and remind them regularly about it.

"Growing up in the country, I always felt an affinity for the underdog. Consequently, I look at every customer who walks through our door as being just as good as any other customer, regardless of how much money he has or what position he holds. I have preached to our people that we run our company like a private bank for anyone and everyone. A central concept of our company is we must know our customers. It is a cliché to say, but absolutely true, that our relationships are what define us. We therefore are focused on the basics of good behavior: stand up, call people by name, dress appropriately, and so forth.

"Another very important goal is we teach our folks not to try to sell any products or services, but we try to find out what products or services the people want and then try to help them if we can.

Looking back at it, I could have done things differently, but the thing that saved us was embracing constant change, constant growth, and believing the growth would continue way far down the road. That requires finding the right people, letting them do the job like they think it should be done, and keeping our eyes on the long view, paying attention to every detail along the way, and keeping on.

"Since we intended to build the company to provide service for the long pull that required us to spend the money necessary not only to get the right people, but to invest in the infrastructure that would support our effort. And we have designed products and services that are simple, straight forward, understandable, and reasonably priced. We judge ourselves first on our success in servicing customers, second in servicing the community, and third on providing our shareholders with a decent return. Of course, these are inextricably bound. We believe our bank's effort justify our customer's confidence."

Those who succeed know the importance of **now**, because this is the only time we can, to some extent, control our life. Those who continually try to reconstruct the past, fail to realize there is no way of changing the past; we can only profit from our experience. Everyone fails at some point in their life and the wise person learns from their mistakes. Failure, fear, unfair circumstances, and uncertainty prevent us from going forward and achieving what we can achieve. Life does not stand still, we either proceed or we regress, but we never stand still. We must be willing to use our mind and talents always and in all places. We cannot afford to wait for others to do for us what we can do for ourselves.

Doing all we can, with what we have, where we are guarantees that we will move forward in a positive and productive way. Every day is an important day and should be used in positive ways. This is the reason a "Life Purpose" is a necessity for one who desires to live a fulfilling and meaningful life. Without some idea of a worthy purpose, our life is essentially meaningless. To live without a purpose is to live with hopelessness and fear, and often with thoughts of self-destruction. I have counseled dozens of individuals who were hopelessly burdened with self-doubt, fear, frustration, and a sense of personal guilt, and helped them realize that feelings such as these are not unusual. Most of our negative feelings are the result of our attitude, and expecting others to do for us what we are unwilling to do for them. Doubt and guilt are the byproduct of selfishness and greed. We will never feel guilty about helping others.

It is good to take stock of ourselves from time to time and evaluate the many things for which we should be grateful. While many individuals spend years trying to understand why past circumstances have brought them to where they are without a satisfactory answer, the Apostle Paul advises us to forget the things that are past, and reach for our highest calling. Today is far more relevant to our future than yesterday. The past has given us experience and knowledge that will help us become what we are capable of being.

When we do all we can with what we have, we can rejoice in the here and now. Even minor successes can bring us pleasure. A well-written memo or a well-kept lawn can be satisfying accomplishments. Too many people overlook their smaller deeds as being unimportant, but several small successes can make our days more satisfying and fulfilling. Look back over your life and you will see diplomas, trophies, visible awards, and notable achievements. Those things are worthy of respect, but the spaces between are filled with accomplishments for which we may not give ourselves credit. Pastor, author, and filmmaker Bishop T. D. Jakes said:

"THERE ARE NO COLLEGE COURSES TO BUILD UP SELF-ESTEEM…IF YOU DON'T GET THOSE VALUES AT AN EARLY AGE, NURTURED IN YOUR HOME, YOU DON'T GET THEM."

Wherever you are is an excellent beginning for building faith in yourself and increasing your feeling of self-worth. As Muhammad Ali once said, "It's the repetition of affirmations that leads to belief, and once that belief becomes a deep conviction, things begin to happen." Such determination can erase years of negative beliefs, destructive thoughts, and fear-filled expectations. As a person created in the image and likeness of God, you are immensely valuable when you do the best you can with what you have for the benefit of others. As you value yourself and your life's purpose, you become the person you were created to be.

As we honor and respect ourselves, inevitably we treat our family, friends, and neighbors in the same way. Even a small child can learn to respect himself or herself and show respect for others. Those who hold fast to the convictions in which they believe, despite the challenges and hardships they face, become heroes to those they encourage and inspire. Doing all that we can with what we have for the benefit of others, can be a virtue of heroic proportions. You and I are responsible for the position we hold in other people's lives, and in the future this truth will be the same, for as we give, so shall we receive, as long as we live. England's late Prime Minister Margaret Thatcher said:

"DISCIPLINING YOURSELF TO DO WHAT YOU KNOW IS RIGHT AND IMPORTANT, ALTHOUGH DIFFICULT, IS THE HIGH ROAD TO PRIDE, SELF-ESTEEM, AND PERSONAL SATISFACTION."

This should not be postponed. Today is the day to enter the high road, the day to do our best in whatever we do. There is no need to wait for circumstances to change, or to improve ourselves. That is the beauty of doing all we can, with what we have, where we are **now**.

This paradigm offers substantial rewards. It is a proven remedy for clinical depression, which has risen to epidemic levels in America today. Millions of people seeking relief from such personal demons as burnout, anxiety, sleeplessness, addiction, or extreme fatigue, turn to entertainment, pornography, or pharmaceuticals to ease their pain. These self-prescribed solutions lead to the death of the spirit, as well as death of the body. Fifteen minutes devoted to the simplest task will do more to improve one's outlook than any prescribed anti-anxiety pill. It is the mind that controls the health of the body, and the spirit that controls the health of the mind.

Use the here and now to the maximum of your ability and you will be at peace in the knowledge that you have done your best. By doing our best at whatever we do, we improve our physical health, as well as our mental and emotional well-being. When we neglect ourselves, our duties, or obligations for even a day, we feel a sense of deprivation and guilt. The great pianist, Ignace Jan Paderewski said:

"IF I FAIL TO PRACTICE FOR A DAY, GOD KNOWS IT. IF I DO NOT PRACTICE FOR TWO DAYS, GOD AND I KNOW IT. IF I FAIL FOR THREE DAYS, GOD, I, AND THE WHOLE WORLD KNOWS IT."

Even if we think we are stuck, we do not stay in one place. Our lives, our inner selves, and our performance either moves backward or forward. We never stand still. Each day provides us a realistic choice of options.

When that choice creates a struggle within us, the choice is critical. We move in accordance with our beliefs, our desires, and our visions. Bad moods, annoying people, and unforeseen trials and tribulations rule us or we overcome them. As we learn to overcome the struggles we face, we strengthen our resourcefulness and our character. We strengthen our relationships as we broaden our abilities to render greater services.

A mid-level executive in his fifties was offered a job promotion in another city. He did not want to move because of his two sons, who were nearing high school graduation. Because he did not want to uproot his family, the father found himself jobless and discovered it would be difficult to find another position at his age. As months passed, his savings were depleted, the family sold a car and lived on his wife's part-time earnings. That year he and his sons mowed lawns for a living. Eventually their situation changed and one of his sons spoke of that summer as one of the best in his life.

"Dad taught us how to work and made us grateful for every job," he said.

Whereas the father considered those months when he could not provide adequately for his family to be extremely painful and humiliating, his attitude taught his boys that all work holds dignity and they should be grateful for each job they completed well.

This man did not enjoy where he was during that time, but for his family's sake, he resolved to do all he could with what he had each day. His sons respected their father and told him so on many occasions. The father's appreciation for his wife and children grew and made him feel, in his own words, "like a millionaire." There are times none of us would return to, if given a choice. But if we are honest, we will usually we look back on those difficult periods as blessings and times of growth. When we use where we are in a positive and productive way, we will turn our struggles into triumphs and our weaknesses into strengths.

As we invest our time and effort wisely, our personal and business assets grow, at times gradually, but there is always a measure of growth. This is the reason our good efforts invariably affect others in a positive way. None of us were designed to be self-contained individuals; we were intended to have lives that influence and bless the lives of others. Only the limitations we place upon ourselves will inhibit the flow of our personal influence.

We all have experienced periods of self-doubt, depression, anxiety, fear, or other negative emotions that reduce our courage and confidence. Chief among these impediments are anger, resentment, and unforgiving judgment. Any of these can severely inhibit our positive attitude toward our life. It is up to us to recognize anything that prevents us from living a fully productive and useful life. **Now** is the operative word that brings success, substance, and significance into reality. Believe in yourself as you are now, where you are today, and fully appreciate the value of each hour and each day. Your wealth is within you and in the talents you possess, and will increase in proportion to your confidence in yourself and your faith in the power that gave you your life.

If where you are now does not fit your vision, makes you uncomfortable, or promotes your desire to move somewhere, anywhere, possibly you have been given a divine sense of discontent for a reason. A young woman who for years had been addicted to drugs awoke one day in a moment of lucid thought, and said, "I am too good for this. I don't want this kind of life anymore." That strong realization and declaration marked the end of a dangerous lifestyle. There was no rehab center, no counseling, and no period of withdrawal. Her brain told her a truth so powerful that she believed in herself and recovered by herself. God acts in strange and mysterious ways.

Sometimes people believe that their life is only important to themselves and to no one else. If that were true, they would not be here. But even a few moments of casual thought will reveal the names of many who care for us, value us, need us, and love us. No one on earth is completely isolated, even at the South Pole! I have visited that magnificent place, where despite the harshest of conditions, life, learning, and experimentation constantly changes and is vitally interesting and important to the rest of the world. If you are alive and breathing, where you are now matters to others as well as to yourself. Make the most of today and tomorrow will be better.

An extreme example of equanimity at a pivotal moment concerns Thomas A. Edison, who one night saw his laboratory, full of expensive equipment and 30 years of recorded research, go up in flames. His son Charles searched for his father and found him standing near the inferno.

Edison asked his son, "Where is your mother? Find her and bring her here. She has never seen anything like this in her life and never will again." The next morning Charles found his father surveying a huge stretch of fresh ashes. The inventor commented, "Disaster is good. You get rid of all mistakes and start over."

Perhaps more of us should build a figurative bonfire and toss our foolishness, pride, excuses, and mountains of other mistakes onto the pile. This might be one way to visualize a glorious ending to everything we do not want in our lives anymore. The wonderful thing about today is the fact that it came freshly packaged and ready to enjoy. The outdated, stale, and useless parts of life can and should be discarded. As we all know, Thomas Edison rebuilt, restored, and triumphed over what might have devastated others. That is the reason he was one of America's greatest men. As philosopher and psychologist William James once said:

"BELIEVE THAT LIFE IS WORTH LIVING AND YOUR BELIEF WILL HELP CREATE THE FACT."

A school teacher in America dreamed of going to Europe, but believed her circumstances would never allow it. She thought about London, Paris, Vienna, Rome, the islands of Greece, and the enchantment of Spain. It was all so far beyond her grasp. The year she joined a class about dreams, her belief system changed. Others showed ways to attain what she hoped for, ways any well-educated American could utilize. She could become a tour guide. She could gather a group of students and parents for an educational trip and thus earn her way. She could become an *au pair* in a city of her choice, where parents wanted their children to improve their use of English. She could stay for a year teaching English as a second language.

The important part of these ideas is the fact that the would-be traveler needed to begin now to study Europe, gather facts, investigate possibilities, and firm up her plans. Dreaming is worthwhile and necessary, but now is when the dream begins to become reality. The school teacher has visited countless wonderful places in Europe and acquired many new friends as she went from place to place. Her realization that now is the moment in which to make any dream begin to manifest itself has guided her life from that day forward.

Your dearest dreams, hopes, and visions could begin to happen now, if you decided to ask a question, place a phone call, or revisit an old friend. When you do your best, with what you have, where you are, your life becomes increasingly significant, as you place greater value on the potential it contains. All that really matters to any of us has been distilled within the thoughts contained in our mind. Where we are now is our appointed place to be until we know otherwise. At this moment, where you are holds immeasurable value in the context of life.

A nursery school child told his mother about a little girl he did not like. "She is a wrong kind of girl," he explained to his mother's surprise. "She wastes her picks," he said. It seems that each child, in turn, was given a choice of the next activity and this little girl never made the right choice.

"She says 'play outside' when it's raining, or 'rhythm band' when the other class takes a nap. She wastes her picks."

The mother, intrigued, asked whether adults wasted such opportunities. As he saw it, this happened all the time. Dad could wash a car but preferred to do something else. Mom bought groceries nobody wanted—flour, baking powder, eggs—things nobody found interesting. He declared he would never grow up to waste any of his "picks."

Too much work and too little enjoyment is what many of us experience where we are now. There is a balance in each person's life that can create refreshment, excitement, new learning, and deep enjoyment where we are, when we learn how to live in the moment. In a sense, we are continually rebuilding and polishing and admiring what we have been given thus far. This engenders the kind of thankfulness and gratitude, encouragement and praise that turns the most ordinary person, place, or circumstance into something extraordinary. This blend of mind and will, emotion and spirit, is the ultimate place in which we all should live today. This is a divine ideal, scarcely visualized and hardly ever obtained, yet available to each of us if we will open our mind to the possibilities that are within our grasp.

Our Creator, who is eternal, has given you and me the creative abilities to turn times that most would call unproductive or not worth remembering into times of immense importance and eternal value. This gift of useful time passes all human understanding, yet those who attempt to live fully in that space called "now" achieve a sense of security, gratitude, pleasure, and excitement about life that any of us can envy. These eternal assets can be yours and mine. They are here for us now in the place where we are.

> *"KEEP YOUR DREAMS ALIVE. UNDERSTAND TO ACHIEVE ANYTHING REQUIRES FAITH AND BELIEF IN YOURSELF, VISION, HARD WORK, DETERMINATION, AND DEDICATION. REMEMBER ALL THINGS ARE POSSIBLE FOR THOSE WHO BELIEVE."*
>
> —GAIL DEVERS
> OLYMPIC GOLD MEDALIST

CHAPTER 15

When We Take the Initiative

AT ANY MOMENT when an opportunity arises, an inner feeling pushes us to take the initiative on behalf of ourselves or others. When we do our best, with what we have, where we are, our next move might seem obvious and comfortable, because we are prepared to the best of our abilities. Webster defines initiative as: "The ability to assess and initiate things independently; the power or opportunity to act or take charge before others do." When things seem unsettled, incomplete, or deficient, there may be little comfort in the situation, but we must take the initiative nevertheless to act upon our best judgments.

That's where I was in the autumn of my 25th year. My ailing father, with my devoted mother, had moved into that abandoned, primitive farmstead 12 years earlier, and I, at age 12, became their main source of labor. For more than a dozen years, the three of us sacrificed and toiled until the Triple J Stock Farm had become a fine, restored, and greatly respected farm. Then disaster struck, when our registered herd of dairy cattle was destroyed by disease, and we lost everything we had worked for during the 12 previous years. I was tremendously depressed by our hopeless situation, but took the initiative to do what could be done. I had to leave the farm to find a way to make a living, support myself, and pay my debts.

I well remember driving away from the farm in the new car our banker had loaned me the money to purchase. I was leaving Backus, Minnesota, for Texas, where I would start a new life and hopefully a profession. I drove along that first day with my mind fixed on the road, but that night in a $7.00 room in the Bluebird Motel, I faced my doubts, debts, and deficiencies. I had little education, no college degree, and no job experience. I had to find a place to stay and a job immediately. I owed the mortgage on our farm, the full payment for the new car, and the $300 our banker loaned me to live on until I found work. Knowing I also needed to support my parents and myself, I felt fearful and overwhelmed. Despite my fears, frustrations, and my need for guidance, I was inspired to write a Life Plan that was based upon my faith that God would guide me.

That night as I wrote that Life Plan, I expressed my hopes and desires, and outlined my future accomplishments for the next 40 years. The plan seemed unimaginable, but the act of writing that plan confirmed my lifetime commitment. Every aspect of that visionary plan eventually became a reality, and far more was achieved than I could possibly imagine on that lonely night in the Blue Bird Motel.

Initiative should not be taken lightly or easily dismissed. I believe God motivates us when we are ready. Ideally, we are ready whether we know it or not. In my case, the decisions I made and the steps I took seemed overwhelming. Such moves can become normal events, no matter their size or scope. The ones who care about us will do what they can to help us. For example, our banker, who also owned the local Ford dealership, loaned me all the money to purchase a car and gave me $300 to live on with only a promise and a handshake. He said, "Pay me as you can. I have faith in you and I believe you will succeed."

Sometimes from where we are we see an opportunity but hesitate to take advantage of it. We may feel that it's a small thing and will not matter much one way or the other. When I wrote my Life Plan, I believed that it would be possible. I believed that the help I needed would come to me as a result of my faith. I found a job in Dallas, Texas, that enabled me to develop my abilities and talents, and established a profession that built upon my natural talents and abilities. I met a man who taught me how to invest what I earned in a wise and conservative way that enabled me to benefit from my earnings and increase the value of my time and effort.

At the appropriate time, through a friend, I met the woman I married, and as a result of my savings and investments, was able to offer the security she needed to establish her professional endeavors. All of this took place because others believed in me and in my efforts and initiatives to produce positive results. I had a vision of a fine home when I had nothing but hope, but I believe with the lessons I learned on the farm I could take small homes and make them better through my own efforts, sell them and buy larger homes, until I could have the home I wanted. This was my commitment to do all I could, with what I had, regardless of the circumstances and the struggles required. Nothing is impossible when you are committed to do all that is possible, whatever that might be.

Whenever we take an initiative, almost certainly we will deal with doubts, speculation, and some degree of fear. Where we are at that moment may not feel stable or secure, but when we form the habit of doing all we can with what we have, we produce the foundation for a well-considered next move. Sometimes that move will come as a very humbling experience, and other times as a great opportunity.

A retired National Football League player, divorced and penniless, was so financially destitute that he applied for a job as a department store clerk. This was the lowest time of his life. The one-time football legend was now older, paunchy, and showing signs of too much alcohol. He had lost so much that he felt there was not much he could live for and no reason to live. To his surprise, the department store hired him immediately, but he never worked as a clerk. During the holiday season, the ex-hero was moved from department to department throughout the store, where he greeted customers, chatted with fans, and autographed his pictures. As it turned out, where he was at that low moment in his life brought him back into public attention and he was offered several good jobs. He got his life back because he took the initiative, humbled himself, did his best, and was grateful for the opportunities he was given.

The well-planned and well-executed career goes from stage to stage, with each new experience opening new opportunities for strengthening abilities gained from past experiences. Each new initiative will instill new confidence in the man or woman who, with due consideration, good advice, good thinking, and worthy motives, moves to the next step. When such plans work well, it is not usually due to independent thinking, but positive thinking from many sources and many opportunities.

The ability to take the initiative can begin even before we start school. Parents who encourage children in this way, especially those who set the example before their sons and daughters, are guiding their children into leadership traits and away from impulsive, selfish reactions. Nothing is more important to children than the noble character of their parents, and the worthy efforts of their parents who teach them how to live a life of substance and honesty. Nothing will take the place of a noble, honorable, trustworthy character within a sincerely committed individual. Time tells all things and reveals all persons.

Initiative requires a movement and sometimes that movement seems to be a backwards step. I remember the printer I worked with in Little Rock, Texas, a man I admired for his excellent work, friendly personality, and good character. I even invested money in the expansion of his business, only to see the man and the business go bankrupt. It was a bitter lesson for me taking the initiative to invest in someone I believed in, but necessary for us both. I eventually began to hate him, but through prayer could forgive him; whereas he, feeling deeply regretful over his dishonesty, promised to repay me and followed through with his commitment.

Later, when he took a job as a print salesman, he excelled because he knew every aspect of the printing business, could help his clients receive excellent work at a good price, and, above all, was known for his honesty and good character once again. This man no longer owned a business, but his initiative brought him into a much more lucrative and successful career. He and I each learned much from the initiatives we took. For my part, the lesson I learned has stayed with me: always be ready to forgive.

In cases of broken relationships, like the one I just described, where we are is troubling. None of us can continually manage to take positive steps forward unless we will initiate reconciliation where we are with what we have. If there is tension and difficulty when we are encountering problems, we must organize our priorities and evaluate our options. When someone disagrees with us, it seldom matters who is right, who is wrong, or who must have the last word. The wise person knows how to say "I am sorry," "I might be wrong," or "I was wrong. Please forgive me." After the restoration, right and wrong usually sort themselves out and are forgotten.

In the workplace, the best initiative often is to remain calm while others may remain angry. The one who decides on positive neutrality, with a refusal to take sides, almost always settles the matter. There are certain people in every organization or community who lead because of their refusal to create an uproar, engage in disputes, or cause dissension. That is why they are leaders. "Blessed are the peacemakers," Jesus said, and while this initiative often is difficult, it is always right.

"THE MAN WHOSE LIFE IS DEVOTED TO PAPERWORK HAS LOST THE INITIATIVE. HE IS DEALING WITH THINGS THAT ARE BROUGHT TO HIS NOTICE, HAVING CEASED TO NOTICE ANYTHING FOR HIMSELF."

C. Northcote Parkinson, the British naval historian and author, is credited with the above words. Surely such a man as he describes has not stopped to consider where he is. We all know paper-shufflers, those who have settled exactly where they are, whether they like it or not.

By well positioning ourselves where we are now, this makes us able to take our personal initiative to a higher level. It also makes us eligible for the opportunity offered by someone who has witnessed our personal strength, integrity, and character. It's like the little girl who packed her suitcase, saying, "I'm not going anywhere now, but someday I will." With that attitude, the grown-up girl will go as far as she desires.

During the early 1980s, film and television star Gary Sinese initiated Vets Night, which provided dinner and free performances for Vietnam veterans. This action countered the hostility towards those men returning from that war and began a wide span of proactive celebration of our troops that continues to this day. This was many years before his name was recognized as the actor who was nominated for an Oscar portraying a man who loses his legs in the jungles of Vietnam. After Sinese played that role of Lt. Dan Taylor in *Forrest Gump*, the hit movie helped raise the nation's consciousness of how much we owe our fighting men and women. It also formed an enduring connection with servicemen and women throughout the military community.

In 2004, Sinese formed the Lt. Dan Band, which has entertained troops at home and many dangerous areas abroad. The band performs some 30 shows per year, supporting wounded heroes, Gold

Star families, veterans, and troops around the world. The actor's initial reaction toward soldiers returning from an unpopular war caused him to initiate activities which year by year grew exponentially. He is applauded not only by the military, but by families and citizens worldwide, and is regarded as a prime example of what one man's vision and initiative can do.

But it doesn't take the popularity of a movie star to achieve outstanding success with an imaginative initiative. For example, a six-year-old boy manned a lemonade stand to raise money for his father's cancer treatments. His initiative netted $10,000! A college student who enjoyed late-night karaoke, sponsored an evening's entertainment provided by more than 300 singers. Their enthusiasm raised nearly $6,000 for Boston Children's Hospital.

When a mother opened her 12-year-old son's closet door, a shower of books, games, and toys cascaded from a top shelf. "I outgrew those things," the boy said. "I don't need them anymore." When the mother suggested he should give these good items to younger kids, he reminded her he was among the youngest in their subdivision. The woman remarked to a newspaper columnist friend that there probably were hundreds of other outgrown toys in children's closets and the writer posed the question to the public: Was there a specific need in the community for good, used playthings?

Dozens of phone calls assured the writer that others wanted to contribute. A Catholic church offered warehouse space for distribution purposes and neighbors agreed to canvas city blocks for donations. Eventually, the warehouse was crowded with outgrown tricycles, skateboards, training bikes, and every indoor and outdoor game imaginable. The 12-year-old and his father helped distribute toys and playground equipment to every community center in the city. Volunteers even removed swing sets and reinstalled them in public playgrounds. One woman's sensible question brought on a chain of initiatives city-wide. The act of giving and helping distribute made a deep impression on the young boy, whose possessions had started the drive.

Samuel Dash, the Chief Counsel for the Senate Watergate Committee during the Watergate scandal, once said:

"WHEN YOU BELIEVE IN WHAT YOU'RE DOING AND USE YOUR IMAGINATION AND INITIATIVE, YOU CAN MAKE A DIFFERENCE."

That is the truth behind the Komen Race for the Cure, organized in 1983 by a woman grieving for her sister, lost at an early age to breast cancer. The original race in Dallas, Texas, involved 800 cancer survivors and supporters. Today, it's a global movement with more than 150 races, one million people, and participation on four continents! It has raised millions for breast cancer research.

Thousands of similar ideas, initiated by private citizens, celebrate and elevate millions of lives. One person's idea, one person's initiative, can grow to massive proportions. It is never too early or too late in life to initiate something needed and something productive. A woman in her 80s, still supple and agile, decided to use her apartment's basement for a new enterprise. Once a professional ballet dancer, she offered dance classes on Saturday mornings for any person, of any age, who wanted to learn ballet. Her neighborhood responded enthusiastically and soon children and adults paid $1.00 per lesson, with many beginning a serious study of dance. The teacher regained her star position as mentor, teacher, and friend to one of her most beloved and valuable audiences.

Most of us wonder why someone doesn't...or if someone tried... or if people would only...? When small dissatisfactions make us impatient, it's a signal for us to use positive and productive initiatives. Doubt, fear, and inactivity have never produced anything for anyone. The initiative we plan and execute for the benefit of others, our neighborhoods, or our city, could change the lives of far more people than we realize. As one man said, "Before I die I want to teach at least one person to read." After his retirement, he taught adults to read in evening classes. When many read well enough to attain paying jobs, the volunteer teacher was overjoyed. Those of us who have a similar lifetime desire to help others, owe it to ourselves and to the world to use our initiative to achieve worthy life-changing results.

Every day of our adult life we have the opportunity to help someone, give someone encouragement, or give someone the love they need in the way they need it most. Take the initiative to give what you can and be the person you most desire to be.

> ***"IT IS NOT OFTEN THAT A MAN CAN MAKE OPPORTUNITIES FOR HIMSELF. BUT HE CAN PUT HIMSELF IN SUCH SHAPE THAT WHEN OR IF THE OPPORTUNITIES COME HE IS READY."***
>
> *— Theodore Roosevelt*

CHAPTER 16

Financial Freedom

IT HAS BEEN decades since I left the family farm at the age of 25 and began my first job in the wider world of business. I was deeply in debt, responsible for supporting my parents and myself, and repaying the farm mortgage and other debts we faced. I remember well my feelings about my tremendous financial obligations and the money I owed, not only for my new car, but also the $300 the banker had loaned me to live on until I could find a job. All of this combined was not only overwhelming, but burdened me with fear beyond anything I have ever experienced. I am now grateful that I can remember those burdens of fear and hopelessness, because many of those I counsel today experience the same self-doubts, fears, and uncertainties that I faced, without knowing how they can overcome their financial and emotional problems.

In my own case, when I started my professional life in Little Rock, Arkansas, I needed a place to live close to where I was working. Shortly after I arrived, I saw a sign in front of a small house near my office that said "For Sale or Rent." At that time, I had saved a total of $2,000. When I asked the owner the price, he said $5,000. I agreed to pay the asking price, gave him $2,000 for his equity, and assumed the existing mortgage. That evening I slept on the floor of my first home, a 600-square-foot shelter close to the railroad tracks. I immediately proceeded to paint the house inside and out and build a small back porch. My total cost of materials was under $400 and my equity was greatly increased through my vision and efforts. Within less than a year I sold the house for $7,500 and bought another two blocks away.

This was the beginning of several acquisitions, each more profitable than the one before. I continued this process of buying houses and making them homes over the following six years, until I had a fine home in a fine neighborhood, totally free from debt. Through stringent saving and employing myself as the builder, painter, roofer, and landscaper, I established my capital fundraising profession, repaid all our family debts, and was able to support my parents within a period of six years from the day I left the farm.

Most of us accept the truth that man does not live by bread alone, but also recognize that without sufficient funds, we are at a substantial disadvantage. There is a vast difference between money and wealth, a difference important for us to understand. Money is currency that can be used to purchase what is needed or desired. Wealth represents ownership and the possession of that which is owned. Wealth can be material, psychological, or spiritual and deals with who we are, as well as what we possess in monetary or material form.

Money and wealth have a tremendous influence on our lives. Where we are at any time is often measured by where we are financially. We want to move, but believe we cannot afford it, or we have money to invest, but can't seem to decide how to use it. Money affects our life in many ways. It determines how much we can participate and how much freedom our life offers. As the famous Norwegian poet Henrik Ibsen, known as "the father of realism" said:

"HOME LIFE CEASES TO BE FREE AND BEAUTIFUL AS SOON AS IT IS FOUNDED ON BORROWING AND DEBT."

For one who began their adult life with neither money nor wealth, I feel qualified to share the values of each with you. One who does without appreciates the value of what they possess. Time has proven to me, and no doubt to you, the financial and psychological burden debt places upon an individual. Doubt and debt are co-workers in the destruction of the individual, who otherwise could be successful. Debt destroys confidence and doubt destroys ambition.

Few people fully understand the statement: "The rich get richer and the poor get poorer." The reason the rich get richer and the poor get poorer is the simple fact they continue doing what they have been doing. Credit card use provides an example of where one's money goes. Those who maintain unpaid balances month after month pay a high premium for the money they spend. Few take time to total their credit card interest to know the actual price of their purchases.

Per the American Credit Card Debt Statistics, as of May 2016, the average American family owed $5,700 in household credit card debt. The average debt for balance-carrying households was $16,048. The total outstanding U.S. consumer debt was $3.4 trillion. When it comes to credit cards, 38.1 percent of American households carry some credit card debt and those with the lowest net worth carry the highest credit card debt of over $10,000.

Many people begin their adult lives often necessarily in debt as they begin the habit of living beyond their means. This is so easy to do and becomes a continuing lifestyle habit, with few thinking much about it. Recently, a young woman told a television interviewer that she handled the money during the first years of her marriage. With a new house and all it required, she found herself with $40,000 of credit card debt. She said her husband forgave her, then said, "We'll work this out together."

The couple sold their home and saved more than $1,000 a month with the purchase of a smaller home in a different neighborhood. They sold their expensive car, made a household budget, and worked extra hours. She said, "We sold a lot of stuff, but we're living better than before." The lessons the couple learned by the time they discovered the benefits of financial freedom turned this young wife into someone who helps rescue others drowning in debt. She has become an advocate for financial freedom and has influenced many others to follow her example. Incidentally, she no longer uses credit cards.

Some people buy luxuries when they should only purchase necessities. The person who has "champagne tastes and a beer budget" often sees himself at a higher financial level than he occupies. Instead of putting money aside for a rainy day, he thinks about high-end vacations on a sunny island beach. When the rainy day comes, as it often does, this person feels dismayed and indignant that his lifestyle has been interrupted. Immediate gratification is practiced by far more people today than ever before, and the price for self-indulgence is greater than ever before.

Once the "need" for luxuries and pleasures one cannot afford begins, it usually results in burdensome debt and financial bondage. The person who has victimized himself in this way is often caught in the unpleasant trap of consumption. Ask the woman who was convinced her job required her to wear designer clothing, which had to be replaced each season. Listen to the man who thought he had to drive a car which suggested affluence to impress his clients if it was worth the price.

Some people spend with no thought of saving and fail to invest for their retirement years. A businessman in his sixties awoke to the cost of failing to save and remarked, "I must work for a living if I am to live." Most people consider retirement at age 65 to be a God-given right, yet only a small percentage have a well-thought-out plan for their retirement. Year by year the cost of living rises and life spans increase. Too often our senior citizens fear they will outlive their money. If we took a census among the people we know, most of us would be astonished how few live with financial security and freedom.

These conditions are the result of the habits we form. Poor habits will always produce poor results. We become poor because of the habits we form and the habits we allow to control our life. I know well of what I speak. I began my adult life without any form of financial resources. However, I deliberately formed the habits which produce success and wealth. When we focus our thoughts and intentions on the financial goals we desire to establish, and form the habits that enable us to achieve them, our objectives will be reached and we will be free to become the person we are capable of being. As Pastor Joel Osteen said:

"IT'S GOD'S WILL FOR YOU TO LIVE IN PROSPERITY INSTEAD OF POVERTY. IT'S GOD'S WILL FOR YOU TO PAY YOUR BILLS AND NOT BE IN DEBT."

No matter where we are in life at this moment, we can form prosperity-building habits and eliminate the debts that destroy our potential. Only positive thinking, planning, and positive efforts can accomplish this objective. Unfortunately, debt usually fosters a negative mindset. For better or worse, we are all creatures of habit. Like the young woman described above, we can change our habits and begin to prosper. We can know a new form of freedom the moment we decide to accept and conquer the financial challenges we face by saving and investing and living beneath our means.

One of the gratifications of my current life is seeing the many whom I've counseled over the years develop personal strategies and sound habits that have enabled them to acquire financial security. Some of them began the process during their later years, and thus could acquire the security they had never enjoyed. As a means of encouraging those whom I counsel, I stress the fact that our cost of living doubles every ten years. This is a shocking fact. We cannot expect what we pay today to remain the same in the years to come—it just won't happen that way. Inflation is as certain as death. Everything in the financial world changes.

Each of us has the same amount of time each day. This is one measure of equality we all possess in common. It is the use of our time that enables us to achieve our potential, or fail to achieve what we can achieve. When we do the best we can with what we have, we will increase the value of our time and money and the quality of our life. This habit of doing our best is the foundation of our prosperity and wealth, which includes far more than money or material possessions. No one has an advantage over us as far as the use of time is concerned.

My experience has proven to me that negative people create problems and positive people create solutions, and the difference is controlled by the habits they form and the use of their time. Every positive habit we form makes us a better person. Every negative habit we overcome makes us a stronger person. Every day presents opportunities to benefit from and strengthen our positive habits. Repetition is the soil in which good and bad habits grow, and the more we repeat a positive thought or action, the stronger it becomes. Repetition compounds habits just as time and saving compounds the value of money. Imagine if you will how much time and compounding will increase the value of your resources and your efforts. If you took one dollar and doubled its value annually for 20 years, it would increase to $524,288. Whatever you save and invest wisely will compound in value over time. Remember the wise words of Benjamin Franklin:

"IF YOU WOULD BE WEALTHY, THINK OF SAVING AS WELL AS GETTING."

The average college graduate in 2016 had $37,172 in student loan debt, up six percent from the year before. In 2016, Americans owed nearly $1.3 trillion in student loan debts, spread out among more than 44 million borrowers. Entry-level jobs, where available, often limit a young person's ability to repay more than the interest on these debts, and often not even that. Thus, the burden of individual debt mounts steadily and weighs heavily upon a young person's ambition and outlook. Often such debt inhibits their concept of a positive future.

I can relate to the feelings and fears these young people carry, because my own beginning was very limited and fearful. I used the force of my desires to overcome my limitations, and sought every way possible to free myself from debt. I worked seven days a week and sent half my salary to the banker to repay the money I borrowed to buy a car, pay the farm mortgage, support my parents, and pay their personal loans. My greatest responsibility, and the driving force in my early life, was to free myself from the burdensome cost of debt.

It is important for us to appreciate the position lasting debt can play in our life. It inhibits our freedom and confidence and diminishes our capacity to think positively and creatively. It is an obligation that must be paid regardless of circumstances. This may mean taking a second job, using public transportation, foregoing entertainment and pleasure, and finding other ways to sacrifice to obtain financial freedom and personal security. This form of success is equal to the finest college degree.

Those who achieve success and establish worthy and productive lives, usually discover creative ways to use debt effectively and repay it honorably. Thousands of available college scholarships remain unused. In-depth research for grants, scholarships, and work programs can yield huge benefits for the student with determined initiative. The earlier serious students begin to seek such helpful information, the more likely they are to acquire an education that enables them to become successful. This positive attitude is fundamental to the earning of wealth and the utilization of its potential.

As Thomas J. Stanley and William D. Danko wrote in their best-selling book, *The Millionaire Next Door,* most millionaires don't live in Beverly Hills or on Park Avenue, they live right next door. These wealthy people live in modest homes, drive modest automobiles, live conservatively, and raise responsible children. They invest their money wisely and spend it thoughtfully. Their wealth and success often resides in intangibles such as character, integrity, and honesty. Their family life, church, community involvement, and public service offers them priceless benefits for wholesome living.

Another best-selling book, published in 2002, emphasizes that work is service and that we are meant to serve one another and to prosper. Rabbi Daniel Lapin, affectionately known as "America's Rabbi," teaches on prosperity in thousands of American synagogues and churches. His book titled *Thou shall prosper: Ten Commandments for Making Money,* tells us that the more people we know the more likely we are to find those whom our talents will serve, and thus find personal and financial prosperity.

The Holy Bible teaches more about money and prosperity than almost any other topic, and its principles are deeply rooted in Jewish culture. Rabbi Lapin emphasizes that the talent for wise financial use is not merely a Jewish trait, but their financial superiority is based on principles available to all mankind. In this context, money and prosperity relate to the heart and character of the individual. As Rabbi Lapin wrote:

"FOR THE MOST PART PEOPLE PROSPER WHEN THEY BEHAVE DECENTLY AND HONORABLY TOWARD ONE

ANOTHER AND LIVE AMONG OTHERS WHO CONDUCT THEMSELVES SIMILARLY."

When we do our best with what we have, we automatically find ways to appreciate our assets and diminish our liabilities. We become increasingly mindful of building assets. No matter how little we think we have when we begin this process, it's amazing how rapidly we can increase that small amount when we decide to do so.

Forego a $5.00 cup of coffee before work each morning and save the money. How long would it take to purchase an expensive coffee machine that creates multiple brews in seconds from fresh coffee beans? Each purchase we make is an asset or a liability. The more we recognize this fact, the sooner we will begin to achieve wealth. Wealth is usually acquired over time through the compounding influence of reinvested earnings.

Earnings that compound at the rate of ten percent annually will double in value every seven years. If we invest $2,000 a year for 40 years, and receive an eight percent compounded return, we would have over $500,000 in wealth. Time is the greatest friend of wisely invested money. Young people who are willing to invest ten percent of their earned income over their working life can retire wealthy at the age of 60.

The knowledge of how money grows is of great importance to any person who desires to fully utilize the benefit of time and money. Self-discipline strengthens our character, as well as our financial security. Here are some of the lessons I have learned in the process of acquiring a substantial measure of wealth. I have followed these principles throughout my working life, and have encouraged hundreds of others to follow them as well:

- *Save and invest at least ten percent of your earnings*
- *Invest in a well-managed, no-load Index Fund*

- *Use real estate as an investment opportunity*
- *Always live beneath your means*
- *Continue your education as long as you live*
- *Concentrate your efforts on specific objectives*
- *Never borrow for luxuries or pleasures*
- *Never maintain an unpaid balance on your credit card*
- *Always go the extra mile in rendering your services*
- *Honor your commitments and acknowledge your debts*
- *Follow the Golden Rule*

One of the reasons many people with high incomes are not wealthy is they don't understand how wealth is acquired. Many live from paycheck to paycheck—the more they earn, the more they spend. Of course, the more they spend, the more taxes they pay. Few who work for a salary become wealthy, because of the way they receive their income, and the percentage of taxes they pay on the income they earn. Those who own their business or work for themselves have more opportunities to retain a greater portion of their earnings.

Taxes alone consume 50 percent of the income of a highly paid executive. When taxes are included with high-cost living, there is little left beyond the potential equity in their homes and the diminishing equities in their cars, boats, and other luxury items which diminish in value. Unless one understands the difference between assets and liabilities, wealth will never be achieved, regardless of the amount of money earned. Remember that money represents a means to an end. Money is a tool that can be used to build the life you desire, if you use it responsibly and productively.

The objective in building wealth is to have your assets working for you, and keeping your liabilities to a minimum. In wealth building, self-discipline serves as the Gate Keeper. One of the important traits related to character and the building of wealth is the ability to delay gratification. There is a beneficial, emotional, and practical aspect related to delayed gratification.

The expectations related to your desires can become a strong motivational influence in the acquisition of that which you desire. When you work for something you desire, you will develop emotional energy that stimulates your efforts with a sense of purpose. When you purchase something that you desire with cash, the cost of that purchase is less than if bought on credit. The two major expenses in the average person's life are taxes and interest paid on debt. These two areas of expense consume over 50 percent of the average person's income, and neither produces one cent's worth of equity value.

"So many people live within unhappy circumstances and yet will not take the initiative to change their situation because they are conditioned to a life of security, conformity, and conservation, all of which may appear to give one peace of mind but, in reality, nothing is more damaging to the adventurous spirit," said hiker Christopher McCandless, whose itinerant lifestyle was made into a movie entitled *Into the Wild*. A respectful approach to good personal financial management not only strengthens you where you are, but leads to financial freedom, substance, security, and wealth. This benefits you, your family, neighbors, community, and our nation. With what you have, where you are, at any age, I encourage you to become wiser and wealthier through self-discipline, focused thoughts, worthy objectives, and the determination to do your best at whatever you do.

> ### *"MONEY IS THE CONSEQUENCE OF DOING THE RIGHT THINGS."*
>
> — *BENJAMIN FRANKLIN*

CHAPTER 17

Honest Effort

IT'S EASY ENOUGH to advise a person to, "Do all they can with what they have where they are," but at difficult times in our lives we may resent where we are. Circumstances may be negative and even depressing. A job may seem unbearable and there may appear to be no plausible options. Life throws numerous obstacles in our way, no matter how well prepared or how competent we might be. There are no perfect answers to some of the problems we face, but face them we must to the best of our ability.

Invariably, however, honest, sincere, dedicated effort will eventually turn the tide. For a dozen years of my young life, I worked seven days a week, milking and feeding 25 cows twice each day, every day of the year. In no way could I see this work as my destiny, or even a worthwhile preparation for any form of a better life. Now, from the vantage point of perspective, I realize that this difficult and tedious time of my life taught me the lessons of endurance and faithfulness to family needs, and the work habits which became fundamental to my professional and personal life. Such efforts and struggles which seemed unbearable in many ways, became benefits and have served me well throughout my life. As the late British Prime Minister Winston Churchill once said:

"CONTINUOUS EFFORT—NOT STRENGTH OR INTELLIGENCE—IS THE KEY TO UNLOCKING OUR POTENTIAL."

Most of us are inclined to avoid struggles and hardships. Those who endure them, believing that they have reached a dead end, have two options. They can do all they can with what they have, or they can do everything in their power to excuse their failed performance. Wherever we are at any time is the place from which we progress or regress. Only honest effort can make the difference. Our best efforts breed honesty within our character, nobility within our work, and integrity within our commitments. This may not be exciting, but it is true. The earlier we learn to keep on keeping on with diligence and faithfulness, despite lack of enthusiasm, the sooner we learn to believe in ourselves. Brilliant people whose performance is a flash in the pan achieve applause for a moment, but their inability to persist in their efforts will lead to failure.

The child who is rewarded for good work learns early the importance of good work. Replacing toys on a shelf, emptying a waste basket, or making a bed are not fun, nor recreational, and tend to be uninteresting when done day by day. Therefore, too many parents do not insist that their children, impatient for pleasure, should have to learn the realities of responsibility as soon as possible. Too many view responsibility as something to be avoided. A significant percentage of college freshmen fail and return home. At age 18, many young people cannot manage to get out of bed on time in the morning without someone making them do what they should do for themselves. Unless a child is taught the importance of accepting responsibility, they will suffer inadequacy throughout their life.

School dropouts, failures to report to work, sick days, and a variety of excuses among young adults begin early in the home. The virtue of honest effort takes time, patience, and much repetition in the life of a child or adult of any age. Napoleon Hill, the best-selling author of *Think and Grow Rich*, who experienced intense childhood struggles, wrote the following:

"STRENGTH AND GROWTH COME ONLY THROUGH CONTINUOUS EFFORT AND STRUGGLE."

Where you are may seem meaningless. But look beyond what you see and seek ways to add meaning to your life as you persevere in doing what you must do. As the years have passed, I've discovered that milking those cows at the same time twice each day provided a fine opportunity for practicing my public speeches and developing the ability to express my thoughts with empathy and understanding. At that time, the cows were my audience, and as time passed, thousands of business leaders became my audience, as I sought to fulfill my life's purpose of rendering services that benefited others.

Each of us who learns to enjoy their work discovers a greater sense of significance for their life and the value of a more significant life. We learn how to improve upon, simplify, or save time with certain jobs. We learn how to plan our work, ascertain which aspects take priority, and do all we can to optimize the value of what we do. These useful and productive attributes can produce not only excellent work habits but important character traits as we aspire to reach our greatest potential.

At times when we feel secure, our life will abruptly change. Patricia had a good job and a new condominium when her company merged with another. Within weeks she and several of her colleagues found themselves downsized out of a job. The evening after Patricia received her pink slip she emailed an SOS to a friend, asking her to come help her update her resumé.

The friend said, "Congratulations! You're getting a promotion," to which Patricia replied she had just lost her job.

At that moment, the realization struck her full force and she wept. "I'll lose my condo! Even with severance pay I can only survive for three months." Her credit cards were nearly maxed out, she explained, because it's expensive to furnish a home. As her friend listened sympathetically, Patricia cried harder, exclaiming, "I'll be living at the dump!"

Looking around at the tastefully decorated room, the loyal friend said, "If you go to the dump, you'll have the biggest, best-decorated box in the neighborhood."

The two burst out laughing and got to work. Her exemplary performance in a monotonous job slot and high recommendations by those who knew her work, gave her entrance into a new job that used more of her talents. What began as a tragedy turned into a triumph. She still enjoys her condominium.

We never know the true importance of what we are doing, or the impression it might make on whoever is watching. An honest work ethic becomes a rewarding experience, because it creates within us a greater respect for ourselves. We can't fake this. Our work, of course, is only one measure of our character, but an important one. Whether our assignment requires brains or brawn, either is vitally necessary. A lumberjack is as important as an architect. Likewise, an electrician is as important as an engineer. The builder requires each. The building is only as good as the honest work of each. As the game-winning basketball player and coach John Wooden said:

"SUCCESS IS PEACE OF MIND, WHICH IS A DIRECT RESULT OF SELF-SATISFACTION IN KNOWING YOU MADE THE EFFORT TO BECOME THE BEST OF WHICH YOU ARE CAPABLE."

Honest, committed effort is the only antidote to discouragement. Someone has said, "Discouragement is a favorite tool of the devil." I transcended the long hours of hard work on the farm by reaching out into the wider world through writing and speaking competitions and correspondence with well-known people. I tried to expand my mind by reading great books. I wrote for our local newspaper and, although an introvert living in virtual isolation, challenged myself to enter the 4-H Club public speaking contests. These efforts proved to be immensely rewarding, even enabling me to speak before the United States House of Representatives and the Senate and meet two American presidents before I was 20 years old.

However, I am convinced that the daily discipline of many tedious, tiring, often dirty jobs became the underpinning of my respect for ethics, faithful performance, and problem-solving abilities. I neither desire nor recommend drudgery, but it undeniably provides the impetus to move past where we are today and the sturdiness of character required to take the next step. As French philosopher and writer Antonin Sertillanges once said:

"THE REWARD OF WORK IS TO HAVE PRODUCED IT; THE REWARD OF EFFORT IS TO HAVE GROWN BY IT."

Many lives experience times when every unforeseen circumstance caves in around them and the individual wonders what to do and how to survive. Life is not always fair. Bad things happen to good people, leaving them wondering and bewildered. When life becomes a huge mass of tangled strings, usually the best thing to do is take the nearest string and begin untangling it. Honest effort at this point becomes the most therapeutic way to recover emotionally and allow the mind to sort through present circumstances and create worthwhile priorities. Effort is the key because steady effort generates energy and energy creates the best possible field in which the mind can operate.

We all know stories of individuals who have overcome incredible difficulties and each of these stories involved human effort. Bedridden or wheelchair-bound people who discover the means of helping themselves, whether by intense therapy or by finding ways to work, invariably transcend their circumstances and often heal much faster than those who remain inert. Daily effort, even when efforts seem fruitless, produces patience and prosperity. Patience results in hope and with hope comes a vision of progress, relief, and a strong desire for victory. First, however, one must grab the string and ignore the enormous tangled mess of one's life.

I remember the spring of 1954 when our fine herd of registered dairy cattle became diseased and had to be destroyed. Everything my father, mother, and I had worked so hard to successfully build was destroyed almost overnight. We held an auction and sold everything we could sell. Our farm became inoperative. Physical, ethical, and emotional problems arose immediately—urgent questions which required answers now. Only by the three of us continuing to work steadily, as though everything was normal, did it become possible for me to leave the farm, find a job, and eventually create a prosperous profession. I can testify that only by honest effort, and the resultant hope that comes from staying steady, can one qualify for enough faith to attempt the impossible.

There are countless stories of lives marvelously transformed simply because they knew, without being taught, that sincere effort and honesty of character eventually produce a good outcome. Many of our most famous artists, sportsmen, and business executives have known enormous personal setbacks and persisted, despite trials most people never experience. Overcoming such trials and hardships can amount to heroic self-discipline, perseverance, great faith, and hopeful expectations.

Many such individuals develop an enormous capacity for physical and mental work. General Electric CEO Jeffrey Immelt spent 24 years putting in hundred-hour weeks each year. Starbucks CEO Howard Schultz, since returning to turn around the company, gets into the office by 6:00 a.m. in the morning and stays until 7:00 p.m. Schultz continues talking to overseas employees even later at night from home. He goes into the office on Sundays and reads emails from his thousands of employees on Saturdays. These are extreme examples of intense effort, which few of us feel required to make.

However, very early in life, certain talented people find it necessary to begin regular, daily disciplines far beyond those of their schoolmates. Golf prodigy Tiger Woods, basketball great Shaquille O'Neal, and tennis stars Serena and Venus Williams learned the value of sustained effort in early childhood. Tiger Woods practiced golf strokes daily at age three and sisters Venus and Serena Williams started at ages six and seven. When natural talents in athletics, music, art, or any other area of life emerge, the earlier one channels these forces, the better. For the rest of us, whose talents probably need to be discovered as we move through life, only the combined forces of effort and mental growth produce stages of new awareness and purpose. I know well what is required. During all my high school years, I arose at 2:00 a.m., studied my lessons by lamplight till 5:30 a.m., and then went to the barn to begin my morning chores. In the evenings, I worked until 10:00 p.m. when my chores were completed, before I ate dinner and went to bed.

Think of honest effort and the various creative ways people try to avoid it. Human nature encourages many people to find the easiest way to produce or to postpone production. Laziness and sloth are encouraged by today's epidemic use of recreational drugs, alcohol, and a culture which celebrates and admires the many ingenious methods used to avoid real work. Many admire long hours of diversion the way our parents applauded a good day's work. One squanders, the other produces. The tasks we avoid because we dislike them or feel inadequate to them are the ones that can benefit us the most. Deciding to accomplish or delegate empowers us to go beyond what presently hinders us. "Steady Eddie gets the job done," as the old saying goes. Professional basketball executive and former coach Pat Riley once said:

> *"IF YOU HAVE A POSITIVE ATTITUDE AND CONSTANTLY STRIVE TO GIVE YOUR BEST EFFORT, EVENTUALLY YOU WILL OVERCOME YOUR IMMEDIATE PROBLEMS AND FIND YOU ARE READY FOR GREATER CHALLENGES."*

Honest effort is defined as giving 100% and then 10% more. The word "honest" is described as genuine and authentic. We know when our efforts live up to those descriptions. We all know when we give less. Our earliest lessons in life should teach us to always give our best efforts in our own way: honest efforts and honest speech, attention to duties, self-care, learning, and the many essentials of our daily life. The child comes equipped with all the intelligence he or she will ever need, but must learn early the value of honest effort and responsibility. These lessons increase with every year we live, or decrease if someone implants the notion that the good life means as little effort as possible. Almost any news cycle carries stories of individuals who believe success means pleasure, diversion, and self-aggrandizement. Such individuals often end their lives prematurely. Living without purpose and failure to invest effort into the prodigious possibilities within our life, is too often fatal for those who participate.

A good life, one useful and successful, one that requires substance, offers much of significance to the world. A dedicated, committed life can achieve significance as it eventually touches hundreds, thousands, even millions of other lives one will never live to see. Few people think of how much they are willing to invest of themselves in other people's lives—how much effort in terms of work, helpfulness, compassion, encouragement, and love. Effort in behalf of oneself only leads to the possibilities of money, fame, and personal good fortune. Such effort extended with the purpose of making good things happen for others, as well as oneself, produces exponentially greater results. As Steve Jobs said:

> *"YOUR WORK IS GOING TO FILL A LARGE PART OF YOUR LIFE, AND THE ONLY WAY TO BE TRULY SATISFIED IS TO DO WHAT YOU BELIEVE IS GREAT WORK. AND THE ONLY WAY TO DO GREAT WORK IS TO LOVE WHAT YOU DO. IF YOU HAVEN'T FOUND IT YET, KEEP LOOKING. DON'T SETTLE. AS WITH ALL MATTERS OF THE HEART, YOU'LL KNOW WHEN YOU FIND IT."*

Those people like Steve Jobs, and others described throughout this book, understood that the most honest efforts endow the individual with the joys of discovery, and benefit countless others as their discoveries spread. All of us are explorers. We have an innate need to go beyond ourselves, to build lives that produce legacies for those who follow. Even the simplest lives qualify. The unknown grandmother who trains a future world leader may not have a name that is known to the world, but her efforts enhance the world. To consider our daily duties unimportant is to minimize some of the greatest freedoms given to mankind. To honor all that surrounds our unimportant selves is to honor the worth our Creator placed in us. We should do no less than all we can, with what we have, where we are. Regardless of where we are at this moment, we can and should give our best effort to all we do.

> *"PRODUCTIVITY IS NEVER AN ACCIDENT. IT IS ALWAYS THE RESULT OF A COMMITMENT TO EXCELLENCE, INTELLIGENT PLANNING, AND FOCUSED EFFORT."*
>
> — Paul J. Meyer
> Founder, Success Motivation Institute

CHAPTER 18

Our Place

WHERE WE ARE and what we have determines our position in life and the opportunities that are before us. The place we occupy creates the environment and atmosphere from which our mind, body, and spirit develops, in keeping with our best efforts and intentions. Few people think of the place from which they originated, or the physical place where they find themselves now. Where we are and the atmosphere in which we live influences our health, energy, and the pleasures or displeasures we receive. When we do all we can, with what we have, where we are, we will always influence our life in a positive way. This truth will hold firm under all circumstances. Good begets good just as surely as bad begets bad.

"Home is where the heart is" is an old-fashioned but very true saying. In today's chaotic world, home often seems a launching pad for a restless, striving lifestyle. From this spot, we commute to work, travel long distances, even fly halfway around the world to conduct business, only to return to the place from which we launch our next strenuous efforts. When we return home, often it is to deliver suitcases full of new duties and opportunities. Millions of hard-working individuals in every culture each year seem to try to outdo the past year's exploits far from home base. As Irish novelist George A. Moore said:

"A MAN TRAVELS THE WORLD OVER IN SEARCH OF WHAT HE NEEDS AND RETURNS HOME TO FIND IT."

When we learn the wisdom of doing all that we can, with what we have, where we are, we learn how to successfully utilize our time in order to achieve a more balanced and meaningful life. We learn to balance our mind, body, and spirit within our personal place and continually improve our personal effectiveness. The wisdom we gain from experience allows us to evaluate our position with thoughts and ideas that renew what we see, just as nature itself renews the world in which we live day by day and season by season. Nature is often our greatest teacher.

Everything about nature has been ordered by divine design. Nature's renewal process is steady and continual. The lives of the world's most creative people are ordered by design and are also steady and continual. When we look at where we are and see beauty, order, harmony, and peace, we are well-equipped to operate successfully and effectively. It is important for us to recognize that the atmosphere in which we live affects our mind, thoughts, and physical well-being. We possess an immense number of options, regardless of where we live, whether we are rich or poor, great or humble. Those who continually procrastinate will depreciate their efforts and lose their greater opportunities. Each of us can add to or subtract from our efficiency and productivity, no matter how little or how much we possess.

Even the most apparently oblivious individual understands these principles to some degree. The young woman who saved and sacrificed to buy her condominium understood her innate need for her own place and what her inner self needed to create its ambiance. Women often seem to have this nesting instinct, but men have the same spiritual need in a different way. The importance of our surroundings to our general well-being is well known to color experts and psychologists. Clinics, hospitals, hotels, office buildings, and airports rely heavily on the use of furnishings and especially colors to create a more soothing, inviting, calming, and creative atmosphere. Any of us can use the same principles and increase the value of our own place in the world, often with little effort or expense. As singer David Allan Coe said:

"IT IS NOT THE BEAUTY OF A BUILDING YOU SHOULD LOOK AT; IT'S THE CONSTRUCTION OF THE FOUNDATION THAT WILL STAND THE TEST OF TIME."

When I bought my first houses and began their renovation, I enjoyed painting them inside and out, adding a back porch to one, and learning how to reroof another. I made necessary repairs inside, cleaned the yards, and planted new shrubbery. These efforts in my own behalf did not feel like work but pleasure. Each improvement offered intense satisfaction. These were no Taj Mahals, but they were mine and in their own way gave me as much pleasure as any of the other dwellings I owned. As I have noted, when I began working on these small houses on rather shabby streets, other homeowners began improving their property. Throughout my life, I have noticed that if one homeowner paints his front door or puts sod on his lawn, others on the same street notice and give new attention to their own properties.

There is something about even a small improvement that adds new dignity to where we are. It creates a new awareness and appreciation for what we have, and often a new resolve to move beyond our present environment, if not physically perhaps much more emotionally. When we add anything of value to our home, our life expands because we invite our friends and neighbors to enjoy our home as we mingle our ideas and affection with each other. This is the start of hospitality. Whatever we do that is positive and productive will almost always enhance the lives of others. Unless one is totally possessive and materialistic, one improvement resonates with the next and goes further than we can imagine.

Regardless of the street on which we live, at any stage of life where we are creates opportunities for hospitality. It does not have to be grand or costly, but meaningful. One hostess says she never fails to offer hospitality at least once every week. "Offering a friend iced tea in a beautiful goblet with a perfectly folded linen napkin is just as important as a five-course meal at a fine restaurant." As author Kathleen Norris said:

"TRUE HOSPITALITY IS MARKED BY AN OPEN RESPONSE TO THE DIGNITY OF EACH AND EVERY PERSON. HENRI NOUWEN HAS DESCRIBED IT AS RECEIVING THE STRANGER ON HIS OWN TERMS, AND ASSERTS THAT IT CAN BE OFFERED ONLY BY THOSE WHO 'HAVE FOUND THE CENTER OF THEIR LIVES IN THEIR OWN HEARTS'."

Some of us have lived lives of far too little and also attained far too much. Some, fearful and possessed of a never-enough mindset, continually acquire possessions to the point of inability to use or fully enjoy what they have collected. Mindless materialism that focuses on acquisitions becomes as damaging as poverty and depravation. It is hard for such individuals to know, much less appreciate, where they are. They become victims of consumption and the need for perceived security by always buying more. No one suggests becoming resigned to bad or insufficient surroundings, but rather the realization that whatever we have now, and whatever place we occupy now, realistically is just for now. Better places can be visualized and planned for, while we do all we can with what we have. According to fashion model and actress Amber Valletta:

"WE ARE WHAT WE SEE. WE ARE PRODUCTS OF OUR SURROUNDINGS."

There is much truth to that, though arguably many people rise from poor surroundings into greatness. Bad neighborhoods do not guarantee formation of bad character. But beauty, order, and good design indisputably create a more excellent platform for a successful life.

I have lived in numerous dwellings in various cities during my career and operated from countless, different comfort levels. One thing was consistent in all those moves: when we make our place better, more beautiful, more efficient, and, above all, more personal, we gain a therapeutic sense of mastery and enjoyment. Paint a bedroom or plant a tree and, invariably, our endorphins and enthusiasm increase. Our Creator made us creative. After all, it was primitive man who invented the wheel and discovered how to use fire. We may feel superior to the people who made those great discoveries, but our present state of being should make us desire to go further. As Trinidadian singer Theophilus London said:

"I BELIEVE YOUR ATMOSPHERE AND YOUR SURROUNDINGS CREATE A MIND STATE FOR YOU."

Ask any married couple to list their three greatest desires concerning the home, street, or neighborhood they occupy and these desires are likely to be different. This is good because each usually can have what they see in their mind's eye and, properly executed, the two visions can merge in wonderful ways. I know this to be true because over the years I have seen a wonderful home develop within the empty rooms we first moved into. We all can have surroundings that invite calm and quiet, as well as domestic enjoyment, and expand to offer times of hospitality and celebrations.

Five times a week, I walk two-and-a-half miles through our quiet neighborhood and into my office, or as I call it, my sanctuary. This place not only provides an excellent work environment and comfort for visitors and myself, but it also contains furnishings and objects of art from some of the many countries we have visited. Framed photographs and letters are hung on the walls; my favorite is the wedding portrait of my beautiful mother, whose eyes seem to look into mine whenever I look up from my office desk. The outer office holds the books I have collected and read over the past decades, though today I usually read from my Kindle! This is my personal haven and I am grateful for it each and every day.

    I often find as I counsel or visit with others in my office that the quiet comfort within this special place seems to make people relax and find ways to express their most personal thoughts and emotions. There is an atmosphere that envelops those who enter my office that quiets their restless minds and leads to meaningful expressions of interest and purpose. As much as I enjoy my sanctuary, it pleases me even more to see others enjoy this special place where I feel grateful and creative. I believe the words of writer, actress, and inventor Vanna Bonta express this well:

"THERE IS NO HOSPITALITY LIKE UNDERSTANDING."

Anyone with sufficient means can hire a top interior designer to help them better understand what they need and desire in their surroundings, but I believe it highly rewarding to do much of this exploration oneself. In this way, we learn to know ourselves better, to know what jars our sensibilities, and what offers peace and happiness. When we do all we can, with what we have, where we are, we truly learn more about ourselves and our deepest desires with each year that passes.

    Obviously, we also increase our original investment, as we systematically improve our home or office. The hardware store owner who saw his business failing because long-time customers chose new "big box" stores over his neighborhood place, felt a strange urge simply to paint his store's interior before calling it quits. He told of how his minor investment in paint combined with major determination to restore his property's immediate look of prosperity. He, like many of us, found picking up a paintbrush to be one of the most therapeutic and hope-building actions any of us ever take. His business did not fail, but became renewed.

Just as most of us discover that we can become transformed by the renewing of our minds, it is a physical fact that transformation can be achieved by renewing even the smallest aspects of where we are and where we live. As the businessman mentioned in an earlier chapter discovered, even a sumptuous office becomes transformed when one sets a beautiful, living plant within that space. As he noted, his office came alive.

Therapists advocate such new life for people of any age. Those whose work requires frequent travel often deprive themselves of pets, gardens, or even potted plants. Once they stay home long enough to acquire even one living thing, whether plant or animal, most remark with wonder at how much this vitality adds to their life. Elderly people confined to nursing homes respond with vigor and new joy when therapy cats, dogs, or even a parrot, visit. The man or woman who at last agrees to adopt a stray dog opens his or her door each night to a grand reception and instant love.

Our spirits resonate with every living thing around us, whether inside or outside our home. Someone once remarked that a house should always contain a new litter of kittens. Kittens and children create an atmosphere of fun and laughter. Perhaps we can't have those two lively options, but there is also much delight to be found in cutting the first bud on the rose bush we planted last year and watching it slowly open. Life, movement, and joy in our home or office, our neighborhood or community, adds significantly to our purpose and effectiveness. Life engenders life and becomes a continuous motivating force. Does this sound like too large a promise for merely painting a room or planting a bush? Try it and see.

As I step out my front door each weekday and begin walking to my office, I experience a wonderful slice of life that varies from day to day, season to season. There are small children and office-goers to greet, deer, fox, and squirrels everywhere I look, and many other forms of life in the early morning world beneath a sunny sky or brisk autumn breeze. It is under these conditions that I arrive at my office feeling energized, happy, and extremely blessed.

In today's busy world, it's easy to lose contact with the ground under our feet, other creatures with whom we share our world, and the luxurious feeling of belonging in this wonderful life. If we live in one room, we can look out the window and enjoy the view. It's ironic that by the time we can afford to own a grand house within a well-landscaped acreage, many of us have too little time to fully enjoy what we have attained. When we do our best with what we have, success and substance usually follow. If we can appreciate where we are, our gratitude rises as we see the added significance of our efforts and purpose.

As a businessman and lifelong real estate investor, I advocate searching carefully for properties that can be improved, then rented or resold for profit. In today's haphazard housing ethic, many people give little thought to allowing a house to grow steadily less habitable until at last they move into something more attractive. Failure to maintain a piece of property costs far more than most realize, until they have to sell their house at a lower price than they originally paid. This makes no financial sense and it's depressing to think that owners cannot enjoy and appreciate what they have.

Where you are reaps especially good benefits when you consider choosing the right street, neighbors, schools, and public places. When it's time to sell, it's easy to find eager buyers. Live where you are for a few years, however, steadily planting, painting, and repairing, and an attachment grows each year. Then when it's time to sell, you will want the buyer to see the place you love through your own eyes. You hope that what you have created will delight the next person or family. In this way, we bequeath meaningful aspects of our own personalities and sensibilities to others. I began with a small four-room house next to a railroad track in a poor section of town. Within six years I lived in a fine home in the best section of town.

Where we are at any time is too fundamental to our souls to describe. If you think it does not matter, that you can make do under any circumstances, you are mistaken. Your physical environment today affects everything about your life. We are created to know, sense, and appreciate beauty and order. Our brains work best in such environments. Whether it's kittens and children, a library of good books and comfortable chairs, or a basement workshop with tools and equipment carefully stored, your environment describes you and benefits your life.

For our sake, and that of every person we shelter and care for, the place where we are should be considered a valuable key to a valuable life. If you have cheated yourself in this regard, simply do all you can with what you have now and see that where you are rises to meet your expectations. There are too many indifferent attitudes and throw-away houses. For the sake of our street or subdivision, our neighborhood and even our nation, we can all set good examples. Property values will increase, but the added dignity, well-being, and satisfaction within ourselves and others is beyond price. As author Melody Beattie said, "Gratitude unlocks the fullness of life. It turns what we have into enough, and more. It turns denial into acceptance, chaos to order, confusion to clarity.

It can turn a meal into a feast, a house into a home, a stranger into a friend."

"WHERE WE LOVE IS HOME - HOME THAT OUR FEET MAY LEAVE, BUT NOT OUR HEARTS."

— OLIVER WENDELL HOLMES, SR.

CHAPTER 19

Person to Person

WHEN WE DO all that we can, with what we have, where we are, we walk the pathway of achievement, accomplishment, and integrity as we meet and honor other such individuals. The person who strives for the highest and the best always meets others they admire and emulate. The rich rewards of working with and living with such individuals goes far beyond any other kind of success. Charles F. Glass, the author of *Brain Drain, The Breakthrough that will Change your Life,* said:

> ***"SOME SAY IF YOU WANT SUCCESS, SURROUND YOURSELF WITH SUCCESSFUL PEOPLE. I SAY IF YOU WANT TRUE AND LASTING SUCCESS, SURROUND YOURSELF WITH PEOPLE OF INTEGRITY."***

"As iron sharpens iron, so one person sharpens another," according to Proverbs 27:17. When this happens, when we discover another individual whose ideas and imagination inspires ours, our own thoughts and ideals soar, and our spirits combine into more than the sum of their parts. This does not always happen, but such relations should be treasured and honored. The good people in our lives are not there by accident. When we do all we can with what we have, we become persons of substance and character that attract the best in others.

As this book emphasizes, success and substance which is intended for ourselves alone has little meaning or permanent value. The world is full of stories of celebrities or other famously rich and well-known personalities who lead unhappy, even dissolute lives, and die leaving little behind beyond their sensational headlines. The millions of far less unknown people who build lives of consistent and dependable value invariably treasure above all else those people who have encouraged them and applauded their good efforts.

Think about the three most influential people in your life, especially those who have encouraged you the most and helped you to succeed. Abraham Lincoln's sister Sarah encouraged her younger, motherless brother to educate himself. Richard Montañez credits his wife with encouraging him to pray for guidance, and this janitor eventually became a corporate vice president.

Think also of the three most important occasions when your words of encouragement had their greatest influence. A young man dressed in his first tailored suit asked his grandmother, "Do I look like an executive?"

"Of course," she replied. "You are the type. You are strong, wise, and a born leader. Be sure your character always dresses as well as this suit makes you look."

The young man remembered those words and credited his grandmother with his decision to excel in college and succeed in business. A few words well-chosen and spoken at a key moment can literally change a life. As Dr. Albert Schweitzer once said:

"AT TIMES OUR OWN LIGHT GOES OUT AND IS REKINDLED BY A SPARK FROM ANOTHER PERSON. EACH OF US HAS CAUSE TO THINK WITH DEEP GRATITUDE OF THOSE WHO HAVE LIGHTED THE FLAME WITHIN US."

One of the most important moments of my life happened when I was 15 years old. I was toiling long hours, day after day, having left boyhood behind because of my responsibilities on a farm which barely supported our family. That was the day I asked my mother, "What is the purpose of my life? Why must I work so hard from early morning till late at night every day?" As I have said, my mother obviously was prepared for my question, because she knew how I struggled with the long hours of work and the fact I couldn't go to school as the neighbor children did. Her answer has stayed with me all my life: "Ask God to show you His purpose for your life," she answered.

I have prayed this prayer from that day forward: **"Dear Father, help me find the purpose for my life."** It was many years later that I would understand how that prayer was answered, when I began to realize that God's purpose for my life was being formed during those years of privation and endless labor on the farm. Our prayers often inspire our hopes and stimulate our efforts to fulfill the hopes we pray for. The ability to convey our humanity and even our despair to someone who understands and offers encouragement, can restore and transform our life. Such opportunities come to each of us, but the person with a neglected or failing personal life seldom manages to inspire others. As the old farmer said, "You can't pour from an empty bucket." Our habits of doing all we can, with what we have, where we are, give us the emotional and ethical substance which benefits others as well as ourselves.

The late Jim Valvano, who was diagnosed with cancer at age 46, inspired millions as a basketball player, coach, and broadcaster who never gave up. His words and winning attitude affected countless numbers of people who never met him. He said:

"MY FATHER GAVE ME THE GREATEST GIFT ANYONE COULD GIVE ANOTHER PERSON; HE BELIEVED IN ME."

It took decades for me to realize that my own taciturn, demanding, and highly ethical father deserved that same tribute. I did the never-ending, heavy work my father assigned to me and considered him dictatorial. I had to become an adult of several decades before I came to understand what it must have cost my ailing, honorable father to transfer his own duties onto the shoulders of his young son. I respected him always, but not until I became much older did I realize how much he believed in me.

Each of us needs at least one such person in his life. Each of us can relate to someone else, younger or older, with sincere belief that fosters the recipient. There were others in my life whose encouragement I shall never forget: the school teachers who came to our farm on Saturdays to teach and test me, my 4-H Club advisor, our local newspaper publisher, and the banker who believed in me and gave me an unsecured loan. My gratitude for those great people in my early years will last forever, and I will always try to live up to their expectations.

Some who read this may feel they never had anyone to encourage or truly believe in them. Recently, a four-year-old girl was kidnapped and later rescued by the police. They asked her to tell them her name.

"Idiot," she replied.

She knew no other name to answer to and, unfortunately, there are too many other souls lost in a world of hurt and contempt who have no idea that their lives hold value. We cannot always rescue those who are so damaged, yet each of us, at some point in our lives, has at least one opportunity to throw a lifeline to another person. The person whose family for generations has subsisted on welfare can meet by accident another person who inspires them to obtain an education, a job opportunity, or a better neighborhood in which to live. The rescued person eventually may lead countless others out of the same unprofitable lifestyle from which they came. Think about the career criminal who read the words, "Be ye transformed by the renewing of your mind." When his life became transformed, he led many other former criminals into productive, useful, and healthy lives.

We need each other more than any of us realize. As Steve Jobs once said:

> **"GREAT THINGS IN BUSINESS ARE NEVER DONE BY ONE PERSON. THEY'RE DONE BY A TEAM OF PEOPLE."**

The person who does all they can with what they have is instinctively motivated to help others. No one forms a team alone. We unite our efforts by sharing our interest and support with others through our encouragement and recognition. When we are motivated by our desire to give of ourselves to others, we inspire others to do as we have done. As we follow the Golden Rule, we become the person that brings to life the best in others.

If we become a worthy example, we will bring out the best in others. In these days, when angry words litter the social network and destructive actions pervade some of the world's most admired places, those who offer their best can overcome the forces of the most hateful, destructive, and inhuman actions. It is tempting to retreat from the darker streets in our chaotic world, but those individuals who represent a candle in the darkness invariably see their light increase in the lives of those with whom they associate. This is today's challenge, and any person reading these words can decide to become a guiding light to those in need of guidance in the darker times of their lives. As Eleanor Roosevelt said:

> **"WE ARE AFRAID TO CARE TOO MUCH, FOR FEAR THAT THE OTHER PERSON DOES NOT CARE AT ALL."**

The person who sincerely cares about the next person seldom encounters rejection, but more often is rewarded with gratitude.

Psychologists say that loneliness is an epidemic within the United States and that isolation leads to depression and other forms of mental illness. Such isolation, at its core, is selfish, an unwillingness to extend oneself to the next individual. Taken to an extreme, it leads to psychosis.

Fortunately for me, an introvert whose childhood was spent on an isolated farm, my father, a man of few words, prodded me into entering public speaking contests. When I practiced and won, he was delighted, and I now understand why. He wanted me to overcome my natural shyness and become skillful in communicating well with others. Not only did this become a key element in my business success, but it is the source of too many cherished relationships and lifelong friendships to count.

Because of my own experience, I encourage others to desire and actively form attachments with others they admire. Often this makes for business success; always a heart-to-heart relationship with another of any age, race, or gender becomes priceless. I am grateful that my father encouraged me to learn how to speak and relate to others. Without taking person-to-person risks, we lose many of the rewards that come from meaningful human relations.

I think of a man who read my first book, *The Power of Purpose*. He wrote me a letter, saying that his mother had recently died and my written words helped him regain his faith in God following the loss of his beloved mother. At the end of his letter he made a statement I shall never forget. He said I had taken the place of his mother through the feelings I had expressed and the hope I had given him. Imagine what his letter has meant to me? Years later the same man drove the long distance from his home to my office, and shared his feelings about our long-distance connection. This intimate conversation inspired me greatly and relit the flame of my own desire to reach out even more to others.

Episodes like this have inspired me to write similar notes to people whom I may never meet. These are significant milestones in any life, yet it is too easy to overlook them. The worldwide clamor of hateful voices can be overcome by a few well-chosen words from someone with love in their heart, who is willing to share their faith in the power that gave us life. It does not take genius, high education, or psychological training, only a thoughtful mind and a willing heart. Some personalities treat others with pessimism or cynicism, others with optimism and hope. When we choose the latter, our efforts last so much longer. These are our monuments and may persevere for generations. As the Prophet Daniel said:

"THOSE WHO TURN MANY TO RIGHTEOUSNESS WILL GLITTER LIKE STARS FOREVER."

"The fun thing about getting older is finding younger people to mentor," says Mike May. Blinded at age three, May developed the attitude that, "there is always a way." Mike learned early to reach out to others. Never a recluse, he played flag football in elementary school, intramural soccer in college, lived in a West African village, crashed the 1984 Sarajevo Olympics, started four companies, traveled worldwide, and raised two boys. There are those who consider themselves disabled and those like Mike, who because of his blindness, attempted one daring team involvement after another, drawing countless individuals into his circle of success. Overcomers like Mike May not only teach us much about ourselves, but invariably offer the best of themselves to the people around them.

When any of us become physically challenged, we can be tempted to withdraw from relationships. This is the easy way, but the better path is led by people involved in organizations like the Special Olympics and Wounded Warriors. These heroes of any age chose to reach out and move forward. The rest of us need them far more than they need us. Loss of limbs, eyesight, or mobility are tragic, but the loss of the human spirit is deadly. Look to those whose spirits conquer the highest mountains and be inspired to follow such people.

We all need one another and something innate in every human being knows this. In times of great trouble, we instinctively reach out, hoping there's another hand to grasp. Melina Khanagyan, now living in Provadia, Bulgaria, recalls her hometown of Gyumri, Armenia. In her early childhood, the area suffered a devastating earthquake, which destroyed her town. Then war between Armenia and Azerbaijan followed and Melina remembers years of terrible poverty and starvation. Melina said, "Fortunately, I was a child and didn't understand the difficulties of life. Twenty-six years have passed since the earthquake and our town has yet to be reconstructed." Melina now teaches English in a Bulgarian school.

A colleague told her about People to People International (PTPI), an organization founded in 1956 by President Dwight D. Eisenhower. As the Supreme Allied Commander of the Allied Expeditionary Force, General Eisenhower planned and carried out the Allied assault on the coast of Normandy in June 1944 and eventually liberated western Europe. Following an illustrious 40-year military career and his election as President of the United States of America, Eisenhower passionately believed the antidote to war was peace through understanding. Today the organization embraces 160 countries on every continent. When Melina learned about PTPI, she and her colleague decided to form a chapter. She says that People to People "is a longstanding organization spread all over the world that offers kindness to humanity," and it has taught her "...to be more useful to society and people, and to encourage youth to be more creative and to fight for a better future."

Many of us move from city to city or country to country during our lives, arriving in a new area and often knowing no one there.

Usually we become acquainted through school, business, church, or synagogue affiliations, gradually assuming our place in the community. Very often, however, people find it difficult to merge into new surroundings and seem to find it nearly impossible to make new friends or even to answer their own practical needs. At other times, neighborhoods change, leaving one or two occupants feeling stranded and bereft. One woman wrote to a newspaper columnist saying, "You complain about too many holiday parties. Suppose you were in my place, without one invitation ever? I have no friends." That letter engendered numerous notes and cards, which the woman never answered. Parents and teachers often tell children "to have a friend, be a friend." We busy, often too tired adults, need the same advice. As author and photographer Jon Katz said:

> *"I THINK IF I'VE LEARNED ANYTHING ABOUT FRIENDSHIP, IT'S TO HANG IN, STAY CONNECTED, FIGHT FOR THEM, AND LET THEM FIGHT FOR YOU. DON'T WALK AWAY, DON'T BE DISTRACTED, DON'T BE TOO BUSY OR TIRED, DON'T TAKE THEM FOR GRANTED. FRIENDS ARE PART OF THE GLUE THAT HOLDS LIFE AND FAITH TOGETHER."*

Stressful as it is to change neighborhoods or towns, the best help comes from making friends. Time and again, I realize the value of old friends in this situation, as well as the joy of meeting wonderful new ones. Reach out to anyone you desire to know. Write a sincere thank you to someone you admire. In any way that seems natural, move toward the interesting groups or organizations that seem worthwhile.

When my friend Karen moved from Washington, D.C., to a new city, she knew no one except her real estate agent. Once settled, she consulted the yellow pages and discovered an organization called The Living Vine. This group worked with young women in crisis pregnancies, an effort she supported where she previously lived. Karen visited the center and asked if they needed volunteers. She began working in their office and joined their Board of Directors as the recording secretary.

Several months later, the Board opened a thrift shop to help support The Living Vine, and Karen was led to volunteer as the manager. With no previous retail experience, Karen encountered a new world of activity. Eleven years later, she has enlarged her friendships by the hundreds as she assists clients and learns of their problems, needs, and hopes. She has met dozens of other willing volunteers and community leaders. To walk through a door and ask if someone needs help very often leads us into satisfying new roles and valuable new friendships.

There are brilliant "loners" in this world, those who individually work in some quiet space where they can be undisturbed. Some of us might visualize this existence as ideal because we feel hemmed in and surrounded by too many people. The truth, however, is that we simply cannot do all we can, with what we have, where we are, if we must be alone. We are designed and programmed by our Creator to live among others. Our souls require person-to-person contact. To cherish our aloneness seems desirable, but leads to a self-centered idea of success and personal prosperity. Too many people surrounding us can leave little time for in-depth communication with anyone, leaving us feeling just as isolated and lonely as the hermit. As with everything else in life, balance is required. When we become a true friend to ourselves, we are equipped to offer meaningful friendship to others. As one person stated, "Be who you were created to be." That is a portrait of our best self, the one we should seek and desire to offer to the world.

Doing all we can, with what we have, where we are offers our best to the people we love most: parents, spouses, children, extended family, and community. It is the only way to sincerely build truthful and dependable person-to-person relationships. It is that part of ourselves that lives through others, that lives beyond our time, which becomes our destiny and purpose for living. Those are the traits in us which are unique, admirable, effective, and a personal legacy which will last for generations.

> *"ONE OF THE MOST BEAUTIFUL QUALITIES OF TRUE FRIENDSHIP IS TO UNDERSTAND AND TO BE UNDERSTOOD."*
>
> — *LUCIUS ANNAEUS SENECA*
> *ROMAN PHILOSOPHER*

Part Four: At all Times

"The ultimate question of who we are is set before us at all times and answered with every action."

– BRYANT MCGILL

CHAPTER 20

Seasons and Echoes of Life

ACCORDING TO KING Solomon in the Book of Ecclesiastes:

"TO EVERYTHING THERE IS A SEASON, AND A TIME TO EVERY PURPOSE UNDER THE HEAVENS."

An ancient Chinese belief is that each life consists of three seasons. Youth, the first season, is for personal training, character building, and education. The second season is when we enter the world of higher learning, a career or profession, marriage and family, and community outreach. Mankind's third season, the sages believe, is for fulfilling one's dreams.

The best of lives celebrate each season with the understanding of the possibilities that stage of life offers. The earlier a young person understands the value of education and is led to desire it, the more eagerly they pursue their ideas, their interests, and the development of their talents and abilities, and the richer and fuller their life becomes. Parents who allow their children to waste their time and minds, when they are eager to absorb like sponges life's lessons, encourage our next generation to skim the surface of life without learning to accept responsibility, or the need to produce useful and productive efforts. As Robert Lewis Stevenson wrote in *A Child's Garden of Verses:*

"THE WORLD IS SO FULL OF MILLIONS OF THINGS, I'M SURE WE SHOULD ALL BE AS HAPPY AS KINGS."

A diet of shallow entertainment does not produce happiness for any of us, but a life of curiosity and wonders enriches those earliest years with hopes and desires that echo throughout adulthood.

Children can be a parent's best teachers. They describe things as they see them, often stunning adults with their clarity of vision. A woman related to me how she came into her kitchen one morning to find that her three-year-old son had removed every pot, pan, lid, and vessel from all the lower cabinets. These items were spread across the floor. The woman reacted in dismay: "You're old enough to know better than this!" she cried.

"I'm helping you, momma," the child calmly answered. "You need to show me which are the things you never use and I will put them in the back. The things you use sometimes will go in the middle, and things you use every day will be in front."

The project took time, but the boy persevered. When the cabinets at last were reorganized, the mother said, "He did as good a job as a graduate of MIT or Georgia Tech could do! I realized at that moment, I should let him find his own best ways of doing things, and resolved not to impose my methods on him. This was a mind-opening moment for me, as a mother trying to train a preschooler."

Minds like that one deserve to be trained and expanded thoughtfully and generously from the beginning of the child's life. Parents who put their best efforts into the new generation are helping to build future achievers who will make this a better world in which to live. The children of today will be the leaders of tomorrow. As Major League baseball player Sparky Anderson said:

"GOOD SEASONS START WITH GOOD BEGINNINGS."

The privilege of helping our boys and girls begin well triggers in a parent echoes of their own childhood. Unhappy echoes need not guide what is happening today. Those happy ones, however—the celebration of birthdays, summer camp, swimming lessons, or first days of school—become happy traditions. It is never too early to teach children the important lessons they need to become worthy and productive adults. My parents began to teach me such lessons when I was five years old. I learned to clean my room and hang up my clothes, and at six bring them coffee in bed in the morning! Theresa Lewis, author of *Rising Above Adversity*, said:

> **"EVERY NEW SEASON OF YOUR LIFE WILL BE AN OPPORTUNITY FOR YOU TO LEARN AND GROW. DON'T CELEBRATE THE GOOD WITHOUT CELEBRATING THE BAD BECAUSE THEY BOTH WORK TOGETHER TO PREPARE YOU FOR THE NEXT SEASON OF YOUR LIFE."**

Many of us count the middle season of our life as the most important. We have looked forward to certain milestones: a driver's license, college, sport's trophies, graduation, and entering the adult world with every expectation of success and satisfaction. With proper education and training early, most of us look forward to these events as major steps toward that all-important time of happiness. We will meet the right person and marry, assuming we will live happily ever after. We eagerly accept the privilege and challenge of bringing new life into the world, as we celebrate the birth of children. We seldom consider there could be unhappiness or even failure within these major domains of our life. Those things happen to other people.

In this hard-working season of our life, the demands we each face are greater than we expected. I vividly remember my first adult job. I was 25 years old, straight off the farm, with no college experience, little learning opportunity, and the feeling I must succeed, but was far less equipped than others my age. Like many young adults, I had to make up for lost time and opportunity, or so I believed. Anxiety and fear plagued me when I was required to lead highly respected CEOs and business leaders in capital campaigns with huge financial objectives. I was usually a generation younger than the businessmen and women whom I was guiding. I coped with this deficiency with the help of that wonderful librarian, who kept me supplied with books relating to business and personal development. This story is not unusual, as most of us experience major developmental lacks in one form or another. That crucial second season, therefore, allows us to see and conquer those empty places in ourselves. These should not be stumbling blocks, but new opportunities for adding value to ourselves and to the lives of those with whom we work.

Picture an expensive, beautifully engineered, and well-equipped automobile, the most desirable your mind can imagine. That vehicle is your life and you are the driver. You steer that powerful machine down the avenues your mind and heart most desire to travel. Your vehicle moves almost effortlessly with more power than you can use. Your car has perfect brakes, so you can slow down from a cruising speed to a graceful stop when necessary. It accelerates with power, so you can avoid obstacles or deterrents if you know how it performs. You may come to a steep incline, even a rocky mountain, but if you become an accomplished driver, you know how to shift gears and climb as high as you desire to go. Everything, of course, depends upon you, the driver. The one who idles their vehicle at the side of the road will never reach his destination. There is no standing still in life; we either move forward or backward. Author and photographer Janice Dickinson says:

"THE PAST EXPLAINS HOW I GOT HERE, BUT THE FUTURE IS UP TO ME - AND I LOVE TO LIVE LIFE AT FULL THROTTLE."

That portrait of life is often protested by those who believe their life is ill-equipped for the journey I just described. Perhaps they never had adequate driver's training when they were young, or were unwilling to do their best when they began. Whether real or perceived, these illusions color each person's season of life. The important truth is this: seasons change and so can we, no matter what disappointments echo in our mind. As Victor Hugo so wisely said:

> **"WHAT IS HISTORY? AN ECHO OF THE PAST IN THE FUTURE; A REFLEX FROM THE FUTURE ON THE PAST."**

Someone recently advocated that all of us should resolve to do more walking. We should walk away from negative people and negative influences. We should walk away from bitterness, hostility, and unresolved anger. We should walk as rapidly as possible from the scenes which invade our minds and destroy our hopes, ambitions, and efforts. By contrast, we should do more walking toward any person, place, or thing that positively influences our present life, the season of today, for the betterment of tomorrow. Children and young people instinctively hurry toward any source of beauty, truth, or inspiration. In the newness of life, the human spirit begins to blossom or wither. The more truth poured into the mind from the beginning, the more wisdom and substance will be retained for each new season.

Each of us, on reaching the age of accountability, bears responsibility not only for driving our life toward the purpose for which it was created, but to take with us every piece of equipment needed for a fuller, more abundant life. This is not self-seeking, but the absolute reverse. It is our life's overflowing that nourishes not only our life, but the lives of all who enter our sphere of influence. Resolve to live fully within the season you now occupy. This time prepares you for whatever season lies ahead. Make today echo with your abundant resonances. Be aware of each season as you live it, and live it to the fullest of your ability.

Picture yourself in a quiet valley as you ask yourself, "How will I be remembered when my life on earth has ended?" The hills of life will echo their response: "You will be remembered by what you leave behind." Echoes of your life, like the melody of a song, will resound in the memories of those who knew you, what you did for them, and what you meant to them. As a boy I was fascinated by the way an echo increased the sound of my voice as it reverberated from the hills that surrounded me. Now, as I look back on my earliest season, I see that life has an echo of its own that even now reverberates in the lives of others. When our life touches another's life we become a part of their life as they become a part of ours.

In our youth, we are unaware of how our feelings influence those of others, and how our attitudes control our feelings and expectations. During the years that we develop our social, intellectual, and professional life, we usually don't think of how we'll be remembered. We're usually more concerned with the hopes and desires which influence our outlook and the work in which we are involved. This is natural as we struggle to discover who we are and how we'll establish the relationships that will benefit our position and the outcome of our efforts.

Major birthdays will remind us of the season we are leaving or seasons that will soon arrive. As a teacher approached her 50th birthday, she wondered about her future life. She had no idea how to celebrate that Jubilee year, or what meaning this season held for her. She couldn't decide what she really wanted, but the idea of obtaining a doctoral degree kept beckoning.

Her mother told her that she would "be selfish to pursue something that would only benefit her and not her family." To her surprise, the idea would not go away and the woman returned to campus. "A Bobby Soxer again!" she said; she was once more a student.

Her husband and children did not object and the family in no way suffered. As a school teacher, she enjoyed the echoes of happy, earlier experiences, feeling almost a girl again as she studied alongside others a generation younger.

"This season represented another springtime in my life," she said. "I actually relaxed more, dressed more colorfully, laughed more, and enjoyed every moment of my new-found school days."

Yes, we can regenerate earlier seasons, and with adult wisdom relive them to the fullest. We do this when we camp out overnight with our son's Boy Scout troop, coach a soccer team, attend a daughter's dance or piano recital, and in millions of other ways relive, reinvent, and reimagine the best years of our lives. You and I decide the length and depth of each season. At all times we are fashioning our present season and have substantial authority over the outcome of our efforts. Each of us knows what roadblocks our high-powered automobile encounters. One woman said, "If I could go back and become a new parent, I would say 'No' less often. I would let my kids use their own common sense more and borrow mine less. Now that I know them, I realize how often my fears for their safety and well-being made the word 'No' roll off my tongue." A much older woman said, "If I could go back and do it again, I'd give myself permission far more often than I did before."

To live fully is always to realize fully the value of the moment, the time, and the season. In this way, we can become as rich and resourceful as we decide to be. Many of us live with attitudes that restrict many of the pleasures life offers. Perhaps some of these rules were imposed by our parents or teachers, but most likely by ourselves. "A person who has never walked through a mud puddle never understands what it's like to be a boy," one man said. The person who never slides down a steep, snow-covered hill, climbs the highest tree he or she can find, or dives from the highest board at the pool, misses much that is free and exciting in the first days of risking, daring, and learning. Bad outcomes are as valuable as good ones. The kid who watches his father rake a pile of autumn leaves, then dives into the pile when dad's back is turned, carries within him the echoes of autumn's glory, beauty, and the joys of October. Never mind if dad disapproves. Taking the plunge is the part that echoes.

When we do the best we can, with what we have, where we are, the outcome can be prideful and self-aggrandizing, or it can be the reverse. When we truly appreciate that the most ordinary life has its ups and downs, its seasons of quiet or turbulence, and from the farthest end of the spectrum, realize time and again how often various events come full circle, our latter decades will become a season of victories and fulfillment.

Dr. Albert Schweitzer, the German physician and missionary in Africa, described these reflections as "a reverence for life." Dr. Schweitzer lived not only a long life, but an extremely full life. As his biographer described his habit of working full tilt at one project after another throughout a long day, this remarkable portrait of flow is often observed in successfully aging individuals. They have learned to utilize their best ideas and energies in a variety of productive ways, enjoying each pursuit and accomplishment. Anyone observing this season of life among successful grandparents and great-grandparents, easily understands why children, eager to copy and learn, often seem magnetically attracted to the oldest family members.

If indeed life's third season is a time for fulfilling dreams, it begs the question: how many of our best dreams do we lose somewhere along the way? I believe that doing all we can, with what we have, where we are, will always generate expectation and curiosities about what comes next. Such habits create a mind that never degenerates, as science now proves. In fact, the well-used brain continues to grow more effectively if it is used wisely. Laziness or mindlessness can happen at any age, but in our latter years it creates what some call "senior moments." At all times our brains can and should remain dynamically active. The good news is our last years can become our most effective and fulfilling if we choose to make them so.

Today, at 86, I look forward to going to my office each morning and I maintain regular office hours. My office, though I have long retired, is the center of my active life. It is filled with past memories and future expectations. It is where I am writing the last chapter of a life filled with challenges, opportunities, visualizations, aspirations, and the desires of a man who has lived for a worthy purpose. I try to use all of my time for the benefit of others, and this gives me much pleasure and satisfaction. Each person who comes into my office discovers more of himself and more of his potential. This is where I share the fullness of the purpose for which I have lived.

Physical and emotional health problems, in many cases, tempt aging people to assume their functions are too limited to create what they consider a normal life. In their youth they probably would have determined to overcome such disappointments, whereas in later years they lament their losses and make little or no effort to surmount them. The most courageous among us are wise enough not to allow their limitations to stop them. Despite loss of hearing, sight, limbs, or paralysis, we find ways to fulfill our purpose. Indeed, wise people of any age understand the immense importance of their life's purpose. It is the purpose for which they live that makes their life worth living.

I could offer story after story of fascinating individuals whose lives have been changed and hopes have been fulfilled, when they learned to accept themselves and discovered the purpose for this season. Some were in their later years and some were beginning their professional lives. All were in need of love and understanding, someone to confide in, someone who understood them, someone to care about the things they care about, and someone to believe in them and encourage them. This is the reason I keep my office which has remained the same for the past 33 years. My office in Huntcliff will in time become the final chapter of my life's work. It is here that the echo of my life will reverberate through the generations I have served, the lives I have touched, and the hopes I have nurtured.

> *"THERE COMES A TIME IN YOUR LIFE, WHEN YOU WALK AWAY FROM ALL THE DRAMA AND PEOPLE WHO CREATE IT. YOU SURROUND YOURSELF WITH PEOPLE WHO MAKE YOU LAUGH. FORGET THE BAD AND FOCUS ON THE GOOD. LOVE THE PEOPLE WHO TREAT YOU RIGHT, PRAY FOR THE ONES WHO DO NOT. LIFE IS TOO SHORT TO BE ANYTHING BUT HAPPY. FALLING DOWN IS A PART OF LIFE, GETTING BACK UP IS LIVING."*
>
> —*José N. Harris*
> Author of Mi Vida

CHAPTER 21

The Honest Truth

*"This above all: to thine own self be true
And it must follow, as the night the day
Thou canst not then be false to any man..."*

THIS FAMOUS AND often-quoted statement by the character Polonius in Shakespeare's play *Hamlet* is known to most of us and it pierces us with its truth. Most people of goodwill have no desire to evade truth for any reason, yet the single person easiest for us to deceive is ourselves. At all times our honesty is under inspection. In small ways, far more frequently than in huge issues, others notice our attention to truth and honesty. The person who slides the next diner's tip under his own plate does not get away with it. Someone, perhaps at the next table, notices and remembers.

At all times, doing the best we can, with what we have, where we are creates an ongoing excellence in our work, our ethics, and our reputation. To be trustworthy is the hallmark of leadership, because true leaders are honorable servants. These men and women can be counted on, and others around them instinctively know they are worthy of following.

As Mrs. Abraham Lincoln said about her husband, "Mr. Lincoln...is almost monomaniac on the subject of honesty." According to Robert Rutledge of New Salem, Illinois: "Lincoln's judgment was final in all that region of the country. People relied implicitly upon his honesty, integrity, and impartiality." In today's fast-paced world that celebrates "cool" as a substitute for truth, few would understand President Abraham Lincoln, known as "Honest Abe."

Gordon Leidner, a writer for the *Washington Times*, described Abraham Lincoln's honesty in an article he wrote on February 20, 1999. He said:

> "The future president was first called 'Honest Abe' when he was working as a young store clerk in New Salem, Illinois. According to one story, whenever he realized he had short-changed a customer by a few pennies, he would close the shop and deliver the correct change, regardless of how far he had to walk. People recognized his integrity and were soon asking him to act as judge or mediator in various contests, fights, and arguments. As a member of the Illinois legislature and later in his law practice, he took advantage of his reputation for honesty and fairness to help broaden his constituency. His good name helped win him four consecutive terms in the legislature.
>
> "Lincoln soon moved to Springfield, Illinois, and began his law practice, a profession at which he admitted there was a 'popular belief that lawyers are necessarily dishonest.' His advice to potential lawyers was: 'Resolve to be honest at all events; and if in your judgment you cannot be an honest lawyer, resolve to be honest without being a lawyer. Choose some other occupation, rather than one in the choosing of which you do, in advance, consent to be a knave.'"

This is the standard to which we should aspire, and it begins with our personal search, always, for what is true within ourselves and our circumstances. It may be tempting at times to hurry past issues we know we should address, hoping they will work themselves out. Whether at home or in business, we should always position ourselves to lead not only ourselves, but others around us, into stronger agreement on a righteous conclusion. A lifetime of high ethical standards is not a haphazard proposition. We can hold the world's best intentions, but truth and honesty must be sought always, because they do not come naturally.

We arrive in this world naturally selfish and some learn to become quite good at it. If you are as fortunate as I was, you had a father who marched you to the headmaster's office and required you to confess you swapped your chapel offering envelope for one that contained a dollar instead of yours with a quarter in it. It's difficult for an entrepreneurial type such as I was in grade school to pass up such obvious and profitable opportunities, but my eagle-eyed father caught me every time. When I found a dried starfish in perfect condition, and arranged to swap it for my friend's new baseball and mitt, his parents and mine stepped in and the deal was called off. Each time I discovered a wonderful way to increase my fortunes, my parents intervened with emphatic teaching, and not physical punishment. That procedure was reversed only in times when I told a lie. The one thing my father hated most was a lie.

When ethical misconduct is discovered and corrected early in life, it may cost us embarrassment or shame, but nothing compared to the consequences we may experience when we cut corners professionally or lose respect in the eyes of others. Author William Lyon Phelps once said,

"THIS IS THE FINAL TEST OF A GENTLEMAN: HIS RESPECT FOR THOSE WHO CAN BE OF NO POSSIBLE SERVICE TO HIM."

These ideas seem like old stuff, things we learned at home, in school, church, and many other places. How is it then that so many young adults today "go along to get along?" Why is it that whistleblowers in government and industry so often pay high personal penalties? To bring our current society back to the standards our parents and grandparents knew begins with you and me. The days when neither parents nor school teachers tolerated lying seem long gone, as today's well-educated parents brag about their children who have become con artists. Most of us have a bit of that talent in us and we must watch out for it. If we deceive ourselves, as most of us are tempted to do, we risk losing the most priceless commodity our life can offer—personal integrity.

What are my motives? That question is the easiest way for any of us to test our truthfulness in any given situation. The art of persuasion is far different from the art of manipulation. Persuasion draws people together by means of our best efforts to stand for truth. Too many of us have experienced acts of artful manipulation by individuals who offer shades of truth which lure their victims into unhappy and disastrous consequences. At times it is wise to query an individual offering an apparently advantageous proposal as to his or her motives in making the offer.

As someone who for 38 years conducted capital fundraising campaigns for the highly ethical Salvation Army, I knew I had to be scrupulously honest always. Very often, when I entered a new community and solicited volunteers from among the highest local leadership, I invited them to contact CEOs and business leaders who had served as chairmen of my previous campaigns, and who could vouch for my ethical standards. I knew I must guard my integrity and, above all, my conscience at all times and in all places, lest I inadvertently tarnish the reputation and respect of the organization to which I had devoted my efforts and life, The Salvation Army.

As I became more conscious of the value and importance of personal character, I found it necessary to pray for wisdom at all decision-making times. Sometimes we cannot see pitfalls ahead. At times we may be led to trust another person we later discover to be untrustworthy. If our own integrity is kept under Divine guardianship, this may prove to be an opportunity to help another man or woman become the person they desire to be. To seek the right way in life should not make us self-righteous, because each of us is fallible. Rather, the consciousness always that truth and honesty will stand, even when the rest of the world humiliates or forsakes us, provides fundamental structure for our present life and our future destiny.

A child was questioned about a long-overdue book, borrowed from the school library. He maintained that the book had been returned. His mother ordered him to search through every inch of his disorderly bedroom, since the book obviously must be there, but he said he didn't find it. That same week, she noticed the ten-year-old emptying his waste basket into the wire container in the backyard used for burning trash. She hurried into the yard just before the boy was about to drop the missing book into the fire. Their talk afterward revealed that the book was so long overdue that the child did not have enough money in his piggy bank to pay the fine. As they talked, the mother offered to augment his savings and said she'd be glad to accompany him to the library and help him straighten out the matter. With a troubled face and the missing book, the boy set out alone. No ten year old wants his mother with him when he goes to school. That afternoon he returned home, relieved and exuberant.

"She said a ten-cent fine would be enough, because she knew it was an accident," the boy reported. "She said I was a good customer and take good care of books, so there was no damage."

That was the perfect moment for the mother to compliment her son on having a reputation for honesty and reliability. She emphasized the importance of telling the truth at all times, because he would want people to believe him and trust him. Even a young boy understands this profound ideal. The sooner children and their parents resolve to become strict about personal honesty and motivation, the sooner our personal world will become better and easier to navigate.

A similar situation in the business world, where competition often puts down ethics and honesty and engenders gossip about the next person, can become far more complicated. Social media sources provide innuendoes and outright lies about others. Managers read Internet information about employees, and falsehoods can spiral. By contrast, the man or woman who abstains from office politics is often judged and disliked for being too good to be true. Many times this atmosphere can leave us feeling vulnerable and insecure, yet this is where we work and perhaps another job is not easy to find.

In a situation like that, an individual comes to grips with his own motives. Obviously, those who have time to play these office politics seldom do all they can with their assigned tasks. The individual who focuses on his or her assignment, and tunes out the distractions surrounding him, may or may not survive the office climate, but at worst can emerge with self-respect. The question is, how important to you is your own self-respect? If your answer is what I suspect it is, you at all times want to do all you can, with what you have, where you are. This represents Ethics 101. As someone once said:

"WORK AS IF YOU HAVE EVERYTHING TO PROVE, NOT AS IF YOU HAVE NOTHING TO LOSE."

By now you know well that everybody does not respect and admire individuals who at all times stand for honesty and truth. Such people may be labeled as "square," "not cool," nobody you invite for a drink after work. Ridicule and being left out are some of the worst punishments anyone can receive, yet life has a way of coming full circle. When downsizing or some sort of personal misfortune hits the group, the person left out because of his or her high behavioral standards often is the one co-workers turn to for help. For this reason, among others, your right motives and reputation for truth and honesty become an armor for your Self. Nothing lasting can penetrate that armor and, when circumstances change, as they invariably will, you are left standing when others scatter.

At all times the person who seeks personal honesty must measure himself, his thoughts, words, and actions, against the variety of ways in which we can deceive ourselves and others around us. Careless speech and unexamined intentions create unwanted consequences. As the freelance science writer Robin Marantz Henig says:

"THE ENGLISH LANGUAGE HAS 112 WORDS FOR DECEPTION, ACCORDING TO ONE COUNT, EACH WITH A DIFFERENT SHADE OF MEANING: PREVARICATION, MALINGERING, COLLUSION, FAKERY, DENIAL, EXAGGERATION..."

Every one of us has had to backtrack from something we said but did not fully mean, an event especially upsetting to a parent or spouse. At all times when one tries to do their best with whatever they have, such mistakes can easily be overlooked and forgiven. None of us is perfect, and each of us should be prepared to apologize for and rectify the slightest misunderstanding. Our thoughtless words, actions, or inactions can bruise another person. Speaking the truth at that moment heals, whereas turning the situation into a joke can make things worse.

There are multitudes of ways in which the best intentioned among us can deceive ourselves. Russian author Fyodor Dostoyevsky once said:

"LYING TO OURSELVES IS MORE DEEPLY INGRAINED THAN LYING TO OTHERS."

We pretend that our little habits and small failings don't bother others, since our stronger character traits offset them. The more we cling to illusions about ourselves, the less we know of personal truth. We can't relentlessly judge ourselves, of course, and remain productive and healthy, but few of us admit the truth about ourselves, even to ourselves. Psychologists call this a good defense mechanism, but you notice that the heroes of this world, the great men and women we acknowledge, invariably are praised for their true beliefs. Such beliefs come from those who at all times seek the truth.

"CHEATING IN SCHOOL IS A FORM OF SELF-DECEPTION. WE GO TO SCHOOL TO LEARN. WE CHEAT OURSELVES WHEN WE COAST ON THE EFFORTS AND SCHOLARSHIP OF SOMEONE ELSE."

American religious leader James E. Faust said the above words in his sermon entitled "Honesty—a Moral Compass" in October 1996. We begin cheating ourselves early in life and often it seems to work. The more ingrained it becomes, however, the more we obscure our unique path to our personal destiny. Most of us can obtain a considerable amount of success and substance and fool ourselves into believing that this is all there is. The cliché, "Bloom where you are planted," can only be achieved with hard work and persistence. As everyone admires such citizens and applauds them, at times the truth is blotted out. There is something inside successful people that calls them to go further or climb higher, but where they are at that point becomes what is desired at all times.

A successful businessman in his 30s confided to a close friend that his heart's desire had always been to become a physician. But his early business success made him drop the idea and now it was too late. It would take eight years to fulfill that dream and he doubted that he could be accepted into medical school.

"Of course, this is ridiculous," he said, "because by the time I could practice medicine I would be 45 years old."

"You will be 45 in eight years anyhow," his friend responded.

Miraculously, the man was accepted into medical school and enjoyed a well-regarded and fulfilling life in family medical practice. Such stories about hearing one's inner voice and following the truth of one's self-beliefs seem remarkably rare. As someone has observed, it's often not the things we do that we later regret, but the things we fail to do. When we cheat our truest selves, we cheat our destiny. As Rudyard Kipling said:

"OF ALL THE LIARS IN THE WORLD, SOMETIMES THE WORST ARE OUR OWN FEARS."

Seeking the honest truth about ourselves often requires hard work, but makes life infinitely more livable. The work we accomplish with our hands and brains may be effective and excellent, but the work produced from the human heart, and assisted by our best skills and strengths, spills over onto others and benefits more individuals than we can count. This makes the most ordinary life one of beauty and significance. The humblest bricklayer can build a perfectly constructed foundation for a building to be admired for centuries. The painter or carpenter who works at ordinary construction can become an extraordinary craftsman. The well-kept tools and brushes tell part of the story, but the easily measured truth of a building, even a porch or a shed, twice measured and fitted to perfection, will mark the integrity of the builder.

Whatever men and women construct, the fundamental truth of their life's building blocks begins early in childhood. Honesty is not inherited; it must be learned from our parents and others. It is a priceless ingredient of life that each of us should diligently seek to maintain as long as we live. This is the part of us that outlives our physical lives, the part of us we can share with our children and our neighbors will emulate. Jesus said:

"YOU WILL KNOW THE TRUTH, AND THE TRUTH WILL MAKE YOU FREE."

When we know the truth that lies within us, we more easily discern and operate from the truth in other people and other circumstances.

The words written above probably seem all too obvious, but an outstanding number of us overlook the obvious. As Plato said, "The worst of all deceptions is self-deception." His entire work is believed to have survived intact for over 2,400 years and his words are still relevant today. Self-deception is one human pitfall each of us can do something about. More recently, Thomas Jefferson said, "Honesty is the first chapter in the book of wisdom." Fortunately, we are surrounded by men and women we admire, individuals whose wisdom, truth, and honesty lead the way for the rest of us.

The older I become, the more I realize how honesty and truthfulness form the foundation for a successful and useful life. One of the heaviest burdens we can carry is the regret we have for failing to be honorable, tolerant, understanding, supportive, compassionate, and truthful to those who came within the sphere of our influence. When we are true to our noble aspirations and life as we profess to live, we will have no regrets.

> *"IN THE FINAL ANALYSIS, THERE IS NO OTHER SOLUTION TO A MAN'S PROBLEMS BUT THE DAY'S HONEST WORK, THE DAY'S HONEST DECISIONS, THE DAY'S GENEROUS UTTERANCE, AND THE DAY'S GOOD DEED."*
>
> — CLARE BOOTHE LUCE

CHAPTER 22

Obstacles and Barriers

AT SOME POINT in every life, one is likely to face an obstacle higher than they expected, or perhaps a barrier that everyone says cannot be surmounted. These things are real and the facts are true, as far as we are willing to accept them. As Tim Cook, the CEO of Apple said:

"YOU CAN FOCUS ON THINGS THAT ARE BARRIERS OR YOU CAN FOCUS ON SCALING THE WALL OR REDEFINING THE PROBLEM."

Obstacles may seem enormous, but they are life's strengtheners. At all times we can be sure that challenges almost certainly will present themselves. When we habitually do all we can, with what we have, where we are, we are positioning ourselves to overcome anything and everything.

As for barriers—those physical, mental, emotional, or societal walls that cannot be surmounted—there is always proof that someone somewhere has the courage and determination to scale them. This chapter will be devoted to such human ability to surmount the impossible challenges we face. As the old adage goes: "Yard by yard, life is hard. Inch by inch, it's a cinch." And as Walt Disney said:

"ALL THE ADVERSITY I'VE HAD IN MY LIFE, ALL MY TROUBLES AND OBSTACLES, HAVE STRENGTHENED

ME. YOU MAY NOT REALIZE IT WHEN IT HAPPENS, BUT A KICK IN THE TEETH MAY BE THE BEST THING IN THE WORLD FOR YOU."

The worst thing we can do when adversity strikes is to resort to anger, blame, or self-pity. To take stock of what we have where we are and build from that base produces a far better outcome. Obstacles make us rely on our inner resources: the good habits and excellent character traits we have carefully developed, and our positive attitudes gained from past successes, which generate confidence in ourselves and our God-given talents, and in life itself. Obstacles and adversities, in short, can be predicted at any time and in any life. As the Bible says, "The rain falls on the just and the unjust alike."

Here, we intend to consider the best use and strengthening power of personal adversity and even calamity. Some are born into it, with no apparent opportunity for success. The people we visit here parlayed their hope, faith, and opportunities into far more than they dreamed they could accomplish in their lifetime.

There was a 65-year-old man, whose lifetime represented one loss or failure after another. He was five when his father died and at age 16 he quit school. At 17 he had already lost four jobs, and married at 18. He joined the Army at 19, but washed out there. At 20 his wife left him and took their baby. He became a cook in a small cafe and convinced his wife to return home. At age 65, he retired. He considered his lifetime of failures and decided to commit suicide. He began writing his will, but instead wrote what he wished he had accomplished in his life. He knew he was a good cook. He borrowed $87, fried up some chicken using his special recipe, and went door to door selling it. By the age of 88, Colonel Hiram Sanders, famous founder of Kentucky Fried Chicken, had become a billionaire.

In so many inspiring stories, like that of Colonel Sanders, we see a change of mind and heart. The man who saw himself as a classic failure nevertheless had a history of beginning again time after time. Even at the point of suicide, he recognized his one outstanding talent and decided to make one more try at life. His hopes, despite all past failures, this time propelled him far above and beyond a lifetime of obstacles. As Colonel Sanders said, in his own words:

"I MADE A RESOLVE THAT I WAS GOING TO AMOUNT TO SOMETHING IF I COULD. AND NO HOURS, NOR AMOUNT OF LABOR, NOR AMOUNT OF MONEY WOULD DETER ME FROM GIVING THE BEST THAT THERE WAS IN ME"

Legends like that one seldom come along, you might argue, but that is not true. Among the dozens and dozens of extraordinary success stories created by supposedly ordinary people, it's difficult to choose the most surprising and interesting. In every case, however, they illustrate that at all times we should determine to overcome our own particular obstacles. As the sixth President of the United States John Quincy Adams said:

"PATIENCE AND PERSEVERANCE HAVE A MAGICAL EFFECT BEFORE WHICH DIFFICULTIES DISAPPEAR AND OBSTACLES VANISH."

That might not seem the case when you consider Oprah Winfrey's story. She was born to a single, teenage mother, who soon moved north and left Oprah with her grandmother. Except for the farm animals around her, she had no friends. At nine she was raped and at fourteen, became pregnant and the baby died soon after. Despite early childhood neglect and emotional depravation, young Oprah somehow managed to distinguish herself in high school.

Uncertain about her future, she knew she desired something featuring speaking or drama. She was elected school president and because of her public speaking classes, had an opportunity to meet President Richard Nixon. Her career was not easy. She was once fired from a news channel because they said she was "unfit for TV."

Little among the facts outlined above would have predicted that Oprah Winfrey would become the host of the most successful television talk show in the world, one of the most influential women, and North America's first black billionaire. The woman who refused to yield to numerous obstacles and impregnable barriers, has inspired and benefited countless lives. Many marvel at the outcome of a life that supposedly offered few chances. Oprah herself says:

> *"THE WHOLE POINT OF BEING ALIVE IS TO EVOLVE INTO THE COMPLETE PERSON YOU WERE INTENDED TO BE."*

Perhaps, like basketball great Michael Jordan, early in your life people predicted you wouldn't amount to much. Jordan, who is arguably the greatest basketball player ever, was once cut from his high school team. As Jordan says,

> *"I HAVE MISSED MORE THAN 9,000 SHOTS IN MY CAREER. I HAVE LOST ALMOST 300 GAMES. ON 26 OCCASIONS I HAVE BEEN ENTRUSTED TO TAKE THE GAME-WINNING SHOT, AND I MISSED. I HAVE FAILED OVER AND OVER AND OVER AGAIN IN MY LIFE. AND THAT IS WHY I SUCCEED."*

Jordan doubtless would ask us: How many times are you willing to fail? How much do you want to succeed? Such fascinating stories of the human will to overcome obstacles and barriers exist all around us. Michael Jordan's will to succeed seems phenomenal, yet it resides in each one of us if we are willing to use what is built into our DNA.

Rare happenstances in life can prove our willingness to overcome to ourselves and others. Bethany Hamilton was a highly skilled youngster who had surfed from early childhood and understood how to maneuver through the currents and waves off the coast of Hawaii. She was a natural athlete, a winner who delighted in nature and her own physical skills. At age 13, Bethany was attacked by a 14-foot tiger shark while surfboarding. The shark bit off her left arm. One month later, Bethany was back on her surfboard and two years after that, she won her first National Championship. Her bio tells us:

> "In 2007, she realized her dream of surfing professionally and since then her story has been told in a *New York Times* best-selling autobiography and in the 2011 film, *Soul Surfer*. Bethany is involved in numerous charitable efforts, including her own foundation, Friends of Bethany, which reaches out to amputees and youth, encouraging a broken world by offering hope to overcome through Jesus Christ. Bethany's latest project, *Surfs Like a Girl*, a surf film which will showcase her as one of the best women surfers in the world, is set to release in spring 2017. Her greatest joy is being a wife and mother, and she continues to touch and inspire lives globally as a professional surfer and motivational speaker."

No one would want their 13-year-old to encounter such a tragedy, but we learn a lot about a young person's ability and determination to use that great misfortune to challenge themselves and benefit others. As Bethany says:

> ***"COURAGE, SACRIFICE, DETERMINATION, COMMITMENT, TOUGHNESS, HEART, TALENT, GUTS. THAT'S WHAT LITTLE GIRLS ARE MADE OF."***

Fortunately, Bethany Hamilton, child of devout Christian parents, already had strong intimations about her inner resources when tragedy struck. One can only imagine the daring it took when just a month after the attack the young athlete learned to balance herself and adapt her reflexes to the surging waves and moving currents of the ocean she loved. Contrast her resources with those of famous artist Vincent van Gogh:

Van Gogh's father was an austere country minister. His mother was very moody, an artist who transferred her love of nature, drawing, and watercolors to her son. Exactly a year before he was born on March 30, 1853, his mother gave birth to a son, also named Vincent, who was stillborn. His grief-stricken parents buried the child and set up a tombstone to mark his grave. As a result, Vincent Van Gogh grew up near the haunting sight of a grave with his own name on it. It was no wonder that van Gogh was melancholy and exhibited unstable moods during his childhood. He later wrote that his youth was "austere, cold, and sterile." His life's story was one of failure. As van Gogh once wrote in a letter:

"WHAT PREYS ON MY MIND IS SIMPLY THIS ONE QUESTION: WHAT AM I GOOD FOR, COULD I NOT BE OF SERVICE OR USE IN SOME WAY?"

After disastrous attempts at various careers in art sales, teaching, and ministry, he decided in 1880 to devote his life to art. He spent his money on paint rather than food. He lived on coffee, bread, and absinthe, which nourished his disintegration. Around this time, he is also known to have sipped on turpentine and eaten paint. It did not take long before his poor physical health worsened due to his alarming psychological state. He engaged in bizarre acts of physical self-destruction and burned and destroyed many of his paintings out of frustration.

He saw no way to overcome his failings and at age 37 he eventually shot himself. The only painting that was ever sold during his lifetime was sold by his brother. Soon after his death his work began to garner intense critical and financial success. Today, Vincent van Gogh is considered the greatest Dutch painter after Rembrandt. His paintings sell for incredible amounts of money, four of them for more than 100 million dollars. His genius existed from the beginning, but his inability to believe it possible to overcome life's obstacles ended tragically.

A divorced woman with a daughter to support, had no record of achievement in her life. She was living on welfare, struggling to put herself through school, and also trying to write a novel in her spare time. None of these circumstances is unusual, but this story has a fascinating ending. As JK Rowling persisted in trying to leave a penniless existence behind, all the while believing herself to be the "biggest failure" imaginable, something beyond anyone's imagination happened. The author of the *Harry Potter* books went from welfare to become the first writer to earn a billion dollars.

She attributes her eventual success to her failures. As she said in a Harvard University commencement speech, "Failure meant a stripping away of the inessential. I stopped pretending to myself that I was anything other than what I was, and began to direct all my energy to finishing the only work that mattered to me. Had I really succeeded at anything else, I might never have found the determination to succeed in the one area where I truly belonged. I was set free, because my greatest fear had been realized, and I was still alive, and I still had a daughter whom I adored, and I had an old typewriter, and a big idea. And so rock bottom became a solid foundation on which I rebuilt my life."

As you read these stories, it becomes evident that many people, very early, believe they are failures. Because they have tried multiple times and failed at each attempt, they come to believe their personality and very existence represent failure. That idea often leads to suicide. Conversely, others who are told they are no good simply refuse to believe it. Think of Elvis Presley—the King. For some time, his chief fan was his mother. His first recordings went nowhere. When he tried to join a vocal quartet, he was told he "couldn't sing." Right before he became popular, he was told, "You ain't goin' nowhere, son. You oughta go back to drivin' a truck." Elvis Presley fought through all these obstacles and once said:

"WHEN THINGS GO WRONG, DON'T GO WITH THEM."

Another man with little or no discernible talent aspired to a film career. After his first screen test at RKO Studios, an executive noted that Fred Astaire: "Can't sing. Can't act. Balding. Can dance a little." Fortunately, Astaire either knew nothing of that assessment or decided to ignore it. His determination to surmount every obstacle and barrier Hollywood presented made him become one of the top actors, singers, and dancers of his generation.

Probably one of the most misunderstood individuals ever born was a boy named Albert Einstein. He never spoke for the first three years of his life. During his early schooling, teachers assessed him as lazy and predicted he would never make anything of himself. The child had speech difficulties and some teachers believed he was mentally handicapped. He failed school as a teen because he rebelled against his teacher's insistence on rote learning. He tried to test into Zurich Polytechnic, but failed. However, it was noted he did very well in the math and physics section! At that point, Einstein put his mind to the task, attempted once again to enroll in Zurich Polytechnic, and was accepted. A few years later the man once considered "mentally handicapped" earned his PhD. A few years after that he was awarded the Nobel Prize for physics and became recognized as the genius of our modern era. As he stated:

Jack C. McDowell

> *"LEARN FROM YESTERDAY, LIVE FOR TODAY, HOPE FOR TOMORROW. THE IMPORTANT THING IS NOT TO STOP QUESTIONING."*

It doesn't take an Einstein to realize that early beginnings, early opinions, and early failures do not necessarily predict the eventual outcome of any person's life. When Benjamin Franklin was born in Boston in 1706, he was the 15th child and the youngest son of 17 children. The poor family struggled during his early years and Ben left school at 10. At 12, he was apprenticed to his older brother James who owned a print shop. His brother was cruel and, even though James taught Ben the printing business, Ben was often beaten and longed to escape. The boy was a prolific reader and writer, but James refused to print any of Ben's stories, so the boy adopted a pseudonym and wrote a series of witty letters which were printed in James' paper. When his brother discovered the truth, Ben got another beating and he ran away. He eventually settled in Philadelphia, working with another printer.

Like many other runaways who escape to a better place, only to find another tremendous obstacle, Ben Franklin impressed the Governor, who persuaded him to set up his own printing shop. Ben went to England in 1724 to buy supplies, but discovered the Governor never sent his letters of introduction. He was forced to find work in London's printing shops, until he could afford to return to America.

The young man who would later become one of the greatest founders of a new nation also was becoming one of America's earliest and best-known business entrepreneurs. Franklin's prominence and success grew during the 1730s, especially with the publication of *Poor Richard's Almanack*. By 1748, the 42-year-old Franklin had become one of the richest men in Pennsylvania. He turned his printing business over to a partner to give himself more time for science. These pursuits included investigations into electricity, mathematics, and mapmaking. A prolific inventor, Franklin developed the bifocal, the first rocking chair, a flexible catheter, and the American penny. Benjamin Franklin became one of America's most influential founders, helping to draft the Declaration of Independence and the U.S. Constitution.

In an article in *Spending and Saving,* Franklin is described as "a self-made man who believed that success was derived through hard work, diligence, and study. [Though his] own beginnings were of a humble nature, he progressed through entrepreneurship and lifelong learning. He never shied away from being honest about who he was or how he came by his success." As he said years ago:

"HAVING BEEN POOR IS NO SHAME, BEING ASHAMED OF IT IS."

Ludwig van Beethoven's father was an alcoholic and mediocre court singer, who taught his son music with a rigor and brutality that affected him for the rest of his life. Neighbors heard the small boy crying while he played the clavier (a keyboard instrument), standing on a footstool to reach the keys, his father beating him for each hesitation or mistake. On a near daily basis, Beethoven was flogged, locked in the cellar, and deprived of sleep for extra hours of practice. Along with the clavier, he also studied the violin with his father, as well as taking additional lessons from local organists.

Whether in spite of, or because of his father's brutal methods, Beethoven was a musician of seemingly limitless talent. From childhood, he displayed flashes of the creative imagination that would eventually reach farther than any composers before or since. In 1800, while in his 20s, he introduced his Symphony No. 1 and became established as an emerging musical titan. During this same time period, he began losing his hearing and experiencing a loud ringing in his ears. His approaching deafness terrified him, and he considered suicide. He continued to compose, however, creating increasingly more complex works, symphonies which have astounded critics and audiences from that time forward.

Beethoven's deafness was well advanced at the premiere performance of his Ninth Symphony on May 7, 1824. The work he heard in his mind was longer and far more complex than any other symphony before or since and required a larger orchestra. But the most unheard of feature was that Beethoven included chorus and vocal soloists in the final movement. After the strenuous work of conducting so many soloists, singers, and instrumentalists in a unique and major performance, the composer stood facing the musicians, exhausted. He could not hear the audience's thunderous applause. Carolina Unger, a soloist, touched his arm and helped turn him so he could see the audience's wild response. The soloist, like many of the performers and most of the audience, had tears in their eyes as it was the first time that many had realized the extent of Beethoven's deafness. As the composer said:

"THE BARRIERS ARE NOT ERECTED WHICH CAN SAY TO ASPIRING TALENTS AND INDUSTRY, 'THUS FAR AND NO FARTHER.'"

Physical, mental, and emotional abuse of the helpless is one of the most tormenting obstacles any person faces. Arguably, the genius of a Benjamin Franklin or a Ludwig van Beethoven appears too great to be quenched, yet either might have felt justified in deciding at an early age that his life was worthless. Some individuals at that point view normal obstacles as too high and existing barriers as too great to surmount. The two previous stories depict heroes who refused to be forever tormented by past injustice. Young

Benjamin Franklin could not get published, yet is still quoted today. Beethoven could not hear his own sublime music, except in his mind, yet his works still tower above almost all other music ever written.

George Washington Carver was born of slave parents on July 12, 1864, in Diamond Grove, Missouri. His formal education started when he was 12. He tried to get into schools in the past but was denied on the basis of race. No black school was available locally so he was forced to move to southwest Missouri. He studied in a one-room schoolhouse and worked on a farm to pay for it. Carver gained acceptance to Simpson College in Iowa in 1890, and transferred to Iowa Agricultural College, where he distinguished himself and was offered a faculty position after his graduation, unheard of before that time. In 1896 he received his master's degree in agriculture. Later that year Booker T. Washington, founder of the Tuskegee Institute, convinced Carver to come south and serve as the school's director of agriculture.

At Tuskegee, Carver developed his crop rotation method, discovered 325 different uses for peanuts, and found almost 20 uses for sweet potatoes and pecans. Carver did not stop with those discoveries. From discarded corn stalks he found dozens of uses and from common clays he created dyes and paints. Henry Ford, head of Ford Motor Company, invited Carver to his Michigan plant where the two devised a way to use goldenrod to create synthetic rubber and material for paving highways.

For a slave's son in 1864 to dream of higher education would have been unthinkable. Carver focused on his mind, his hunger for knowledge, and his gifts for inventiveness. This low-born citizen utilized some of nature's least-valued products, especially the lowly peanut, to thrust him through barriers few other African Americans had ever breached. George Washington Carver advised industry leaders, presidents, and even stood before kings. There could be no real barrier to such humility, dedication, and genius. As Carver once said:

> **"NINETY-NINE PERCENT OF THE FAILURES COME FROM PEOPLE WHO HAVE THE HABIT OF MAKING EXCUSES."**

Evangelist, international motivational speaker, and *New York Times* best-selling author Nick Vujicic was born in 1982 in Melbourne, Australia, an infant without arms or legs. Nick's parents determined to accept and foster this child, despite inevitable massive challenges. They always told the boy he was perfect and beautiful. They wanted him to experience as normal a life as possible, encouraging him to find ways to do the things that mattered to him. He attended public schools, where other students jeered at him or bullied him.

As Nick grew into adolescence, he wondered more and more why he did not receive a miracle. He couldn't get the haunting question of "Why was I the one born without arms and legs?" out of his head. At one point, he even tried to drown himself in a bathtub. During these formative years of deep soul struggle, Nick read a Bible story about a blind man healed by Jesus. Disciples asked the Lord "Why was this man born blind? Was it his parents' fault or his own?" Jesus replied that it was no one's fault, but the man's purpose was that of glorifying God. Young Nick began searching for his purpose.

A janitor at his high school inspired him to start speaking publicly about overcoming adversity, so at 17 Nick started speaking to small groups of students. At 19, after obtaining a double bachelor's degree, he made the move from Brisbane to Los Angeles, California, where he is now the founder and president of an international nonprofit organization, Life Without Limbs, and owns the motivational speaking company, Attitude Is Altitude. He married in 2012 and the couple has two young sons. Since his first speech, Nick has traveled to over 57 countries, sharing his story with over 400 million people. Nick has a life full of optimism and he shares that optimism with everyone he meets. As he has said:

> *"OFTEN PEOPLE ASK HOW I MANAGE TO BE HAPPY DESPITE HAVING NO ARMS AND NO LEGS. THE QUICK ANSWER IS THAT I HAVE A CHOICE. I CAN BE ANGRY ABOUT NOT HAVING LIMBS, OR I CAN BE THANKFUL THAT I HAVE A PURPOSE. I CHOSE GRATITUDE."*

There are thousands of inspiring stories which make the case that each one of us comes into the world fully equipped to leap over every obstacle and crash through every barrier. Such misfortunes and tragedies described in these stories do not make a person, nor do they have to break a person. As JK Rowling realized when all else about her was stripped away, at the core she had one burning, creative desire and a daughter she adored. As Hiram Sanders discovered, he possessed one positive, creative idea: his secret recipe. The suicidal 65-year-old man parlayed that idea into hundreds of franchises and thousands of jobs for men and women like himself.

We can imagine that such undreamed of riches gained by two formerly failing and penniless individuals might become, in their minds, the Cinderella story of all time. I believe, however, that something far more unimaginably priceless happened to them. By facing once again another of life's obstacles, each discovered the blessing of restoring his soul.

My own life is a typical example of what one can become when they learn to believe in themselves and in the Creator who gave them life. Since I was unable to go to school as other children did and had no formal education, in many ways I had to educate myself. I studied my lessons, learned what great men and women had overcome, and how they struggled to obtain high achievements. I was inspired by their efforts and motivated by their determination. My life was more than difficult, but from such stories such as these I gained the courage to withstand the life I was living.

When challenges, misfortunes, tragedies, and anguish beat us down, life offers us another opportunity to conquer. Obstacles and barriers exist throughout our life. The question is: How much will any obstacle stop me? The truth is such events allow us to learn how limitless we are. Each of us is unstoppable unless we decide to stop. Each of us has the same Creator who gave us our life, our mind, and our spirit. If we will do the best we can with what we have, we will never fail to do what we are capable of doing.

> *"THERE IS NO FAILURE EXCEPT IN NO LONGER TRYING; THERE IS NO DEFEAT EXCEPT FROM WITHIN; NO REALLY INSURMOUNTABLE BARRIER SAVE OUR OWN INHERENT WEAKNESS OF PURPOSE."*
>
> — KIN HUBBARD
> JOURNALIST

CHAPTER 23

Respect and Honor

"RESPECT YOURSELF AND others will respect you," Confucius said. It begins early: respect between parents and children, children and their siblings, authority figures, and friends, as we learn to respect life itself. In today's hurried world, self-respect and respect for others stands out. We notice such people and feel impressed by them. They have a nobility that most of today's society seems to lack.

Any of us can, at all times, manifest the highest respect for our personhood, our work and obligations, responsibilities, and kindness to others. This is the most honorable way in which we can live lives that express high purpose and nobility of character. Where self-respect is lacking, it can be rebuilt in the same way human muscles are strengthened. The habit of seeing ourselves clearly and projecting awareness of ourselves and others inevitably raises the dignity of any other person or occasion. At all times it benefits us to increase our awareness and respect for others. As novelist Laurence Sterne said:

"RESPECT FOR OURSELVES GUIDES OUR MORALS; RESPECT FOR OTHERS GUIDES OUR MANNERS."

A nursing school professor gave his class a pop quiz. The last question read: "What is the first name of the woman who cleans the school?"

Later, one student said, "I'd seen her several times. She was tall, dark-haired, and in her 50s, but how would I know her name?" She had left the last question blank.

"Will the last question count toward our quiz grade?" another student asked the professor.

"Absolutely," said the professor. "In your careers, you will meet many people. All are significant. They deserve your attention and care, even if all you do is smile and say 'hello.'"

That story illustrates the fact that respect is a two-way street, beginning where we are. As we learn, as life goes forward, at all times we should be aware of others around us and treat them with the respect that is due.

"One of the most sincere forms of respect is actually listening to what another has to say," said author Bryant H. McGill. Listening and hearing are vitally important communication skills. Our respectful attention to another person's remarks, even rude or angry words, sets a tone that others emulate.

A legal secretary, who observed many divorce mediations, remarked, "If people simply respected one another, divorce would not be necessary." You may argue that point, but clearly disrespect breaks down human relations. When we respect ourselves too much to show disrespect for others, we are helping the world become more civil, kind, and moral. Think of those in your life for whom you have the highest regard: parents, teachers, coworkers, neighbors, and others, who at all times exhibit not only honesty and high ethical behavior, but respect the intentions of the smallest child or the most grossly incompetent adult. Such people are light in an often rude and darkening world.

A doctor rushed into the hospital after being called for an urgent surgery. The patient's father, waiting in the hall for the doctor, yelled: "Why did it take you so long? My son's life is in danger! Don't you have any sense of responsibility?"

The doctor said, "I'm sorry. I came as fast as I could. Please calm down so I can do my work."

"Calm down? What if your son was in this room right now, would you calm down? If your own son dies while waiting for the doctor, what would you do?" said the father angrily.

The doctor replied, "We will do our best by God's grace and you should pray for your son's life."

"Giving advice when we're not concerned is so easy," murmured the father.

After hours of surgery, the doctor appeared, looking relieved. "It went well. He will live!" Without waiting for the father's reply, the doctor hurried away, saying, "If you have any questions, ask the nurse."

"Couldn't he wait so I could ask about my son? Why is he so arrogant?" the father said.

The nurse answered, tears flowing down her face, "His son died yesterday in a car accident. He was at the funeral home when we called him for your son's surgery. Now he's returning to his family."

Even at such critical times, it's wise not to judge or verbally attack another, because we simply don't know what they are going through. Self-respect requires self-control. It forbids angry outbursts, accusations, and temper tantrums. Self-respect offers that same respect to the next person, regardless of circumstances. In much earlier times, this was called *noblesse oblige*, meaning "nobility obliges," the concept that nobility extends beyond mere entitlements to acts of generosity and nobility toward those less privileged.

As I remarked to a friend recently, "It doesn't matter to me whether I converse with a duchess or a waitress. Each is important in her own right." This illustrates the attitude of *noblesse oblige*. Everyone is worthy of recognition.

When Polish leader Lech Walesa visited Queen Elizabeth II at Buckingham Palace, he was served artichokes. Never having encountered an artichoke before, he began to eat the spiny leaves.

The Queen generously offered, "Why don't you eat the bottom part? It takes so long to eat the leaves." I imagine many of us have had such artichoke experiences!

Each of us needs such grace because none of us is perfect. At all times it enlarges our world as we show respect and understanding for each person God created. If He is not conscious of rank, but blesses each of us with the same amount of favor, we should do likewise. As we respect others, respect for ourselves naturally increases. We want at all times to do all we can, with what we have, where we are, because these are character trademarks. They stamp us as persons of character and excellence, worthy of respect. They enhance the dignity of our personhood, the work we do, and the world in which we live. Self-respect and respect for others is fundamental to civility and our own personal substance and significance.

Many of us are too busy to be consciously aware of people around us who seem unimportant to our lives and goals at the moment. It is easy to overlook the office boy, parking garage attendant, or your child's school teacher, because they have little in common with what you are doing at the time. This is a mistake. Each person within our orbit is important and significant, and the more we realize this the richer our lives become. No person within an organization or work environment, and especially within a family, is less important than another. The German theologian and philosopher Meister Eckhart once said:

"THE MOST IMPORTANT HOUR IS ALWAYS THE PRESENT. THE MOST SIGNIFICANT PERSON IS PRECISELY THE ONE SITTING ACROSS FROM YOU RIGHT NOW. THE MOST NECESSARY WORK IS ALWAYS LOVE."

The story of Richard Montañez, told earlier in this book, has been described as a Cinderella tale about a janitor who became a corporate vice president. Mr. Montañez and his wife had enough self-respect for him to believe his corporate CEO would accept a janitor's telephone call and listen to his idea. Would most CEOs have enough respect for their personnel to accept a phone call from a janitor in one of their factories? This nameless executive obviously felt interested in all the corporation's personnel or he would not have considered someone so untrained to be worthy of his attention.

Respect between two human beings in vastly different positions resulted in a profitable new product for the corporation and a profitable new career track for someone willing to work and learn. This story is inspiring, yet not altogether unusual. Great ideas can come from anyone, anywhere, at all times. The person we might consider the least likely to help us in any way might say or do something that changes our life. When we respect others for character, ethics, and good work habits that is one thing. When we respect them because they are one of God's creations and, like ourselves, of inestimable value, that enlarges our world and increases our soul. As the late actor Bruce Lee said:

"KNOWLEDGE WILL GIVE YOU POWER, BUT CHARACTER RESPECT."

At all times when we respect the work we do, we respect ourselves. Our brains instruct our hands and as they attack the most mundane tasks, jobs well done inevitably increase our self-respect. Others respect us for our work as we learn that even the most menial jobs done well contribute in large measure to human dignity. It was for this reason, I believe, that my father would make me do over any task he considered less than my best. At the time, it seemed unnecessary. Who outside of our family of three would care if the rows of corn I planted were not straight? I neither argued, resented, nor became angry with my father when he asked me to plow up a field of new seedlings and replant them in straight furrows. Wasted effort, some might say, but it certainly taught me the importance of doing things right the first time! From then on, I could survey my work and know I had done my best.

The older one becomes, the more one understands this concept of excellence and the pride of perfection. Doing one's best at all times should not be optional, it should be mandatory. Among all its other virtues, it saves time. No one wants to create a lifetime habit of having to redo tasks that are incomplete, incompetent, or unsatisfactory.

The above words might seem unnecessary, except for the fact that respect for our good work strengthens us throughout our lifetime as we grow more effective and efficient. Self-respect leads us to replace our character defects with better qualities and finer principles.

A young man I heard about years ago was smart, talented, and handsome, but hot-tempered and apt to say hurtful things to others. His concerned father sought to teach him self-control. One day the father gave his son a hammer and a bag of nails. He said to him: "Each time you get angry, take a nail and drive it as hard as you can into this piece of wood." The wood was tough and the hammer heavy; nevertheless, the boy furiously drove three dozen nails into the board the first day. Day after day, week after week, the number of nails used gradually decreased, and the boy started to understand that holding his temper was easier than driving nails into a piece of hardwood. One day the boy didn't need the hammer and nails anymore. He told his father about his achievement.

His father replied, "Now every time when you hold your temper all day long, pull out one nail."

At last the boy could be proud of himself, as all the nails were removed. "You did a good job, my son, but look at the holes that were left from the nails. The board will never be the same. The same happens when you say hurtful things to people, as your words leave scars in their hearts like those holes in the board. Remember, we need to treat everyone with love and respect, because even though you say you are sorry, the scars in their hearts might not disappear." As America's poet laureate Maya Angelou so wisely said:

"IF WE LOSE LOVE AND SELF-RESPECT FOR EACH OTHER, THIS IS HOW WE FINALLY DIE."

When life presents us with embarrassing moments, respect for ourselves and others will save the day. A son took his elderly father to dinner in a fine restaurant. The older man, feeble and apparently nearly helpless, scattered food on his clothing and the table. Other diners obviously noticed, but his son remained patient and encouraging. At the end of their meal, the son led his father to the washroom, where he wiped off the food particles and removed the stains as best he could. He combed his father's hair, straightened his tie, and led him back into the dining room. The entire restaurant seemed to be watching. The son settled the bill and started walking out with his father.

At that time, an old man amongst the diners called out to the son and asked him, "Don't you think you have left something behind?"

The son replied, "No sir, I haven't."

The old man retorted, "Yes, you have! You left a lesson for every son and hope for every father." The restaurant went silent.

To care for and respect those who once cared for us is the highest honor. The dignity within the above story cannot be overlooked. German writer Johann Wolfgang von Goethe said:

"BEHAVIOR IS THE MIRROR IN WHICH EVERYONE SHOWS THEIR IMAGE."

By contrast, consider what happened recently in a Houston restaurant. Parents allowed their three-year-old son to walk around the dining room with no supervision. The boy took a quarter and scratched the walls. He did tic-tac-toe on three walls and disturbed the other diners. *ABC News* reported that "The mishap cost the restaurant $1,200 to pay for the sheet rock repair and a new paint job. The owners also paid their employees for the days off to do the repairs. The family of the boy gave [the restaurant] "a one-star rating out of five on Yelp, claiming the restaurateurs 'discriminate against children.'"

The owner said, "We're not trying to start any 'anti-kid' campaign. We just expect them to behave within the social norm, not invading personal space, crawling under tables, or touching people's stuff." Obviously, it is never too early to be taught to respect oneself, one's parents, and others. As evangelist Billy Graham said:

"A CHILD WHO IS ALLOWED TO BE DISRESPECTFUL TO HIS PARENTS WILL NOT HAVE TRUE RESPECT FOR ANYONE."

Surely all of us have been taught to honor our parents. Such honor is the highest form of respect, involving our willingness to give all we have and all we are to the person or institution we hold in highest esteem. When the late Mary Kay Ash founded her multimillion-dollar cosmetic company, she envisioned an ideal company that would honor each person within the organization. "We treat our people like royalty," she explained. "If you honor and serve the people who work for you, they will honor and serve you."

Mary Kay adopted the Golden Rule as her guiding philosophy, determining that the best course of action in virtually any situation could be easily discerned by doing unto others as you would have them do unto you. She believed that priorities in life meant faith first, family second, and career third. She thought it was important to reward hard workers and gave away vacations, jewelry, and pink Cadillacs to her top performers. With goals such as these to shoot for, her salespeople were the ones who made the company successful. The company was listed in the book, *The 100 Best Companies to Work for in America.* It now employs over 3.5 million people in over 35 countries. May Kay Ash's story illustrates that the honor she gave to her inspired consultants produced rewards of every kind, including astounding financial profits. As philosopher, author and Saint Thomas More said:

"IF HONOR WERE PROFITABLE, EVERYBODY WOULD BE HONORABLE."

We're told to honor those in authority, whether or not we agree with them, because we honor their office and their human responsibilities. We hold certain objects in such awe and honor: our national seat of government, our flag, and our sacred places where fallen heroes are laid to rest. At all times there are moments and words and places we honor as sacred. To not experience such things is to fail to experience life at its highest.

In the United States of America, we honor our unidentified fallen soldiers with a special place of reverence in our most honored of burial grounds: the Tomb of the Unknown Soldier in Arlington National Cemetery. In 1921, we first laid to rest "In Honored Glory, An American Soldier Known But To God."

The most visible honorific symbols associated with the Tomb of the Unknown Soldier are the impressive, specially trained soldiers who guard the tomb. The site is protected by an elite group of men and women who are on duty around the clock, every day of the year, in good weather and bad. They are from the "Old Guard," attached to the Third United States Infantry Regiment. According to the Public Affairs Office of the Old Guard: "The Sentinels who guard the Tomb must be exemplary in discipline, dress, and bearing; thoroughly knowledgeable with the history of their unit, the Tomb of the Unknowns, Arlington National Cemetery (and those interred there), and the U.S. Army; and able to execute a variety of ceremonial rites flawlessly and with precision."

Compare these stringent requirements for the utmost display of honor with what we know about ourselves. Few people become as unwaveringly disciplined and willing to inspire others as they honor fallen comrades. In the end, high respect and honor become the highest form of human character and behavior. We honor those who display such attributes.

One of the most important lessons I learned from my father was to respect the nobility of good, honest, and faithful work, and to appropriately recognize those who perform such work.

> ***"NO PERSON WAS EVER HONORED FOR WHAT HE RECEIVED. HONOR HAS BEEN THE REWARD FOR WHAT HE GAVE."***
>
> — CALVIN COOLIDGE

CHAPTER 24

Be Strong and Courageous

STRENGTH IS A decision. Ideally, we decide early in life to live from a position of strength. This is entirely possible because each of us has the capacity to decide and operate from that decision. Strength produces courage. Courage is one of the greatest and noblest virtues we possess. Courage is directly related to the attitude of strength and one of our greatest sources of confidence. It is the outgrowth of our faith in God and in ourselves.

Learning to operate from personal strength begins early in life and continues year by year throughout our life. As we think more clearly and firmly, our personalities strengthen. We define our personal values; decide what most strengthens and motivates us; and as our physical, mental, and emotional strengths increase, our personal courage inevitably follows. As we accept the fact that we were born in the image and likeness of God, we understand the influence of our creation. Always remember, we become the person in whom we believe as a result of the faith we have in ourselves.

It was a mild May evening in Florida when a stretch limousine occupied by 20 young men and women, bound for their senior prom, screeched to a halt at the side of the road. They had narrowly missed the mangled van ahead of them. The van had been swerving from side to side on the highway, finally landing upside down. The limousine driver raced to help the victims and the formally dressed students quickly followed him.

The panicked passengers were screaming and crying for help as they tried to free themselves from the tangled wreckage. The limo driver kicked out a door to pull some of the passengers out, and one of the young men climbed onto the van to force the sliding door open. There were young children inside, including a small boy who was trapped under one of the seats. The limo driver pulled the little one out and handed him to one of the gown-clad students. The other students continued to help the bloodied and petrified passengers until the emergency medical personnel and policemen arrived. Seven injured passengers were taken to nearby hospitals. The students were shaken but decided to continue to the dance.

As one girl said to a local newspaper, "I went on to the prom and a lot of girls were helping me get the blood out of my dress." On that evening of high teenage excitement and exuberance, these young people became adults, fully aware of their strength and courage. As Greek tragedian Euripides so famously said:

"NOTHING HAS MORE STRENGTH THAN DIRE NECESSITY."

Courage and determination do more to help a person succeed than education or intellectual capacity. Our courage will enable us to overcome most of the obstacles we face. At all times, people who are successful have the strength and courage to do their best and keep on trying until they reach their objectives. Physically, mentally, and emotionally, our only limitations are those we place upon ourselves as a result of our lack of confidence and courage. Our courage resides in the power of our faith in ourselves and our Creator, and that faith is the substance of our strength.

Encourage others to develop their strengths. The little boy with the overdue library book, terrified to face the librarian, discovered strength he did not know he possessed. The businessman or woman faced with the prospect of disagreement or confrontation faces the situation and learns from it. When I faced seemingly impossible tasks, and the need to build confidence in the minds of the doubtful business leaders whose help I needed, my faith in the purpose of our efforts built confidence in the minds of those whose support I needed. Such situations help us develop the ability to inspire confidence and trust. Each decision we make strengthens or weakens our outlook on life. Such strength develops our courage and as Captain Eddie Rickenbacker, the WWI flying ace, said:

"COURAGE IS DOING WHAT YOU'RE AFRAID TO DO. THERE CAN BE NO COURAGE UNLESS YOU'RE SCARED."

In many respects, my life has been driven by the fear of failure. This fear has driven me to do the best I could, with what I had, at all times. This fear of not doing my best was the driving force in all the successes I achieved.

Great stories of heroism often come from terrifying situations. On an ordinary train ride from Amsterdam to Paris, dozing passengers were startled by a gunman opening fire within their car. There was a chaotic, bloody scene aboard the train. Three vacationing Americans on the high-speed train, Anthony Sadler, Spencer Stone, and Alek Skarlatos, immediately sprang into action. Together with a French national and a Briton, they subdued the attacker and immediately became applauded worldwide for their heroism. These young heroes reacted instinctively against the threat of mass murder. Without individual mental, physical, and emotional conditioning, they could not have reacted so swiftly and courageously. As Anthony Sadler, a college student from California, told *NBC's* Lester Holt:

"I DON'T THINK I'M ANY DIFFERENT THAN THE AVERAGE AMERICAN. WHEN PEOPLE ARE FACED WITH THIS SITUATION, I FEEL LIKE IT IS A CHOICE…SHOULD I DO SOMETHING OR SHOULD I GO HIDE? AND I JUST WANT EVERYBODY TO KNOW THAT THEY SHOULD DO SOMETHING."

Strength and courage are not accidental, but aspects of our personalities that we intentionally develop. God's famous commandment to Joshua, "Be strong and of good courage," applies to everyone, because such potential is built within each of us. We can call forth strength as we need it and courage when our noblest instincts take us beyond ourselves. Mark Twain said:

"COURAGE IS RESISTANCE TO FEAR, MASTERY OF FEAR, NOT ABSENCE OF FEAR."

This thought illustrates an incredible story of three men who volunteered for a task that would certainly end their lives. After the 1986 Chernobyl power plant disaster in Russia, radiation emanating from the disabled plant spread and took more lives than ever accounted for. Three team members responsible for the cleanup realized that a pool of water used for emergencies, in case of a break in the cooling pumps or steam pipes, had become flooded with a highly radioactive liquid in danger of exploding. The three suited up in scuba gear and swam into the radioactive waters of the flooded chamber, knowing they would die as a result. They opened the gate valve, which allowed the contaminated water to drain out. Days after reaching the surface all three men succumbed to radiation poisoning and were buried in lead coffins. If not for the bravery of the "Chernobyl Suicide Squad," a thermal explosion would have taken place, resulting in unfathomable disaster.

We can marvel at such courage and nobility, realizing that most of us will never face the opportunity to give our life in order to save unknown thousands. As the Florida teenagers learned, opportunities for bravery can arrive unannounced. The question is, to what extent are any of us prepared?

At all times, in business and civic life, we must be prepared with the courage of our personal convictions. The force of our inner strength, combined with the beliefs that constitute our character, always become our best protection against human evil and failure. A righteous character depends on personal strength and honest conviction. With these attributes, no matter how small and apparently inconsequential the life, that person becomes a winner. It takes courage to overcome past mistakes, failures, or even wrongdoing.

As the lifelong thief I mentioned above learned, it took more courage to ask for forgiveness from the person he robbed, than to enter a dark house and ransack it. It takes more courage, at times, to confront oneself than to swim in a pool of poison. As Christian author Lewis B. Smedes said:

"TO FORGIVE IS TO SET A PRISONER FREE AND DISCOVER THAT THE PRISONER WAS YOU."

We are never alone. At all times, any of us may need someone to help us strengthen our inner self and courageously resolve to change our course. The millions of others who have found the strength to do this give courage to us all.

When we attempt to lead from a position of strength, rather than a position of weakness or self-indulgence, we increase our capacity to face the difficult and challenging problems and opportunities we face. Desiree Lyon, a Texas housewife and mother in her early 30s, never could have imagined that her painful, swollen stomach was the result of a rare disease. Healthy, active, and full of life, at age 35 she was diagnosed with porphyria, a genetic blood disease so unheard of that few doctors could diagnose it. Desiree considers herself fortunate, because she was diagnosed and sent to the National Institutes of Health in Bethesda, Maryland, for treatment.

Each day she visited the medical library, pulling her IV pole with her, and searched for all the information she could find about her condition. Those years before the Worldwide Web's creation, little information was available. Desiree assembled what she found, determined to help herself and other sufferers as much as possible. She volunteered for clinical trials and for several years suffered painful and dangerous bouts of a disease no one knew how to treat.

Desiree was one of the first of her friends to acquire a personal computer and she used this device to search medical sources for further information and disseminate that information to others with what science terms an "orphan disease." There was little or no research money for anything as little known as porphyria, and no government funds available at the time. From her kitchen table, Desiree contacted other patients like herself in various parts of the United States and beyond, patients sent to her by doctors she never knew. Thus began a network of information, advice, and compassion among sufferers of a disease that seemed to have no answers.

From that beginning 35 years ago, the American Porphyria Foundation was born and now extends throughout the world with 8,000 members. Desiree has counseled patients in numerous countries. She has also written a book on porphyria and prostate cancer to raise peoples' awareness of these two diseases. She has attended more medical and genetic conferences than most physicians, has acquired an extensive list of the world's foremost scientists, and has travelled and spoken throughout the United States, Europe,

China, and Australia. Early in her experience, the *New England Journal of Medicine* described her acute, intermittent porphyria as among the six worst in medical literature.

The housewife who pursued these little-known and almost unknowable facts, paid little attention to the times her disease brought her close to death. Nothing slowed her purpose. Beginning with no money for anything beyond medical treatment, no equipment except an early computer and a kitchen table, and no one to help or advise her, one woman created a foundation which has served doctors, patients, and scientists worldwide. The foundation has created huge patient and physician education programs, facilitated eight clinical trials, and started a doctor training program called Protect the Future. This program trains future experts and has one of the most successful media campaigns on television. The foundation helped create the Porphyria Research Consortium, which has raised $10 million in government research grants. Desiree was given the FDA Hero award for her work on the Orphan Drug Act and last year the award in rare diseases. Desiree will only accept an award if it will help promote porphyria awareness.

Desiree's human connections doubtless have become more widespread than that of most CEOs. She has personally advised 17,000 patients one-on-one, either face-to-face, by telephone, or email. She believes her life to be richly blessed. According to author Harper Lee:

"REAL COURAGE IS WHEN YOU KNOW YOU'RE LICKED BEFORE YOU BEGIN, BUT YOU BEGIN ANYWAY AND SEE IT THROUGH NO MATTER WHAT."

There are few guarantees in life, but there are many inspiring people around us who refuse to be stopped by even the worst outlook.

It takes strength to refuse to allow anything to overtake our life, remove meaning from our existence, or create a bitter spirit within us. Financial ruin, a home taken by tornado or foreclosure, business failure, and betrayal by a loved one all can create trauma so severe that many individuals simply give up. They cannot move beyond the circumstances and perhaps have no desire to go forward. That is when we can lend strength to those who feel powerless. At all times we should extend encouragement to everyone around us, because at all times some among us are silently suffering.

Years ago in Germany a destitute mother of four children felt so hopeless that she determined to kill herself. Madame Ernestine Schumann-Heink meant to throw herself and her children in front of a train, but at the last moment her small daughter looked up and said, "I love you, Mamma." Those four words saved the life of one of Europe's greatest opera singers. Born in poverty, she became wealthy and highly acclaimed. The power of anyone's words cannot be overestimated.

Look for ways to add strength to your own life and other lives. This habit is easy enough to form once you adopt the idea. A businessman took his secretary and a part-time clerk to dinner. His secretary noticed that the other woman was carefully saving half of her meal to take home. She whispered to her boss that the woman had a teenage son at home and very little money. Quickly, the businessman asked the woman, "Why not take dinner home to your son? Is there something on the menu he would like?" Later he thanked his secretary for allowing him to do a small kindness for a single mother he hardly knew. This began his search for ways to help that needy woman find full-time employment. His clerk became emotionally stronger because of his kindness and the young boy received nourishment from an interested friend. It is through such small actions that we nourish our own souls and the souls of others.

We seldom hear much about soul health these days, though a century ago the world's best thinkers considered every aspect of the mind, will, and emotions. Our soul is linked to our spirit. As the mind directs our will and emotions, it also directs our brain, which feeds information to every part of our body. Benjamin Franklin was famous for making charts which recorded his progress in instilling desired traits into his life as habits. Each night he would check his day's results, gauging whether or not he lived up to his ideals of diligence, punctuality, courtesy, thrift, and so on.

General George Washington was so highly informed on the importance of honesty, truthfulness, and high character among his Army officers, that he sternly instructed them never to use foul language. He understood the power of words. He knew each man must live up to his highest aspirations in order to win against overwhelming odds. He knew the task demanded the utmost bravery and self-sacrifice. Words that diminished a man would not be tolerated. His own words inspired the coldest, hungriest, and most physically exhausted soldiers to rise to heights beyond themselves. As the American theologian and author James Freeman Clarke said:

"STRONG CONVICTIONS PRECEDE GREAT ACTIONS."

The mind easily can conceive greatness, but as Benjamin Franklin and others knew, it is the will that strengthens us for a higher purpose. Someone once said, "Winners never quit and quitters never win." The human decision simply to persevere against all odds creates far more success than anyone can imagine. It has been said that 80 percent of us quit just before success arrives. The percentage who continue to make additional efforts become a Thomas Edison, Steve Jobs, or perhaps an Einstein! The mind decides to do all one can, with all one has, where one is, at all times. These are just words, however, unless an individual is willing to test the idea and use it effectively. This part of our soul, the will, might be compared to our physical heart. If the heart stops beating, we die. If our will fails, our mind and emotions die. This is one of the most important truths in our life, and to the extent we learn it, we will experience success.

The third element of our soul is our emotions which contribute pain or pleasure to our life. As we move through life, every form of emotion that we experience remains in our subconscious mind, where it influences us throughout our life. There are few who realize how much their emotions guide their lives. As one psychologist put it, "Ask yourself if you are allowing yourself to let your emotions pull you around by the nose." Just as the accumulating knowledge of brain research continues today, many scientists believe that Emotional Intelligence is far more important in guiding our accomplishments than most people realize. Emotional Intelligence predicts whether a person is reasonably happy, relates well to others, does not over-dramatize problems, but faces them sensibly. The emotionally intelligent individual seems to others to be reliable and well-balanced.

The healthy soul, obviously, would belong to the person whose mind, will, and emotions contribute to an orderly, constructive, and satisfying life. Just as some people will allow powerful feelings to dictate their decisions, others may make intellectually strong decisions that dampen their emotions in order to fulfill their purpose. This can be done when a person's will is strong, but the result is seldom satisfying. One's passions, good or bad, power one's destiny. It was the passion of Beethoven which made it possible for him to compose the towering symphonic work that he could not physically hear. As author, businessman, and philanthropist Tony Robbins said:

"PASSION IS THE GENESIS OF GENIUS."

Feelings of lack, need, or shame can motivate individuals to achieve incredible heights, or serve as an excuse for failure. Consider the well-known motivational speaker and author Dale Carnegie, whose book *How to Win Friends and Influence People*, first published in 1936, has sold 15 million copies. The familiar public-speaking course, which preceded the book, has trained millions of students, politicians, housewives, and businessmen and women from that time to the present day. It is sad that the man who taught others to train themselves for success had a deep personal need arising from his feelings of shame about his early poverty. Carnegie was born in 1888 in Maryville, Missouri, to a farm couple who experienced seasons of floods and crop failures. His father at one point even considered suicide as his debts rose.

During his teenage years, Carnegie attended many Chautauqua assemblies and lectures, which brought entertainment to rural communities throughout the country and featured many popular speakers, musicians, entertainers, and preachers. These events inspired Carnegie to begin public speaking in high school. He somehow saw the ability to convey ideas via skilled oratory as a pathway to more achievement. His instincts were correct and as Carnegie moved from one stage to the next, he continued to improve his own speaking and that of others. But poverty seemed to move with him. He could not afford the dollar a day for room and board at the local state teacher's college, so he had to live at home and commute the long distance on horseback. His fellow students looked down on him because of his shabby, ill-fitting clothes. Eventually they accepted him when he started teaching public speaking classes, which were popular with the students. However, when he failed Latin, he left without his bachelor's degree.

He tried one job after another, finally working as a traveling salesman for three years until he earned $500 to go to New York to become an actor, which he discovered he hated. For some time he could not find his niche. Through it all, however, he continued to train himself and others in public speaking, a purpose in which he passionately believed. He received little or no pay for this, but the pamphlet he assembled for his students became the nucleus of the best-selling book which has changed millions of lives. After innumerable efforts and years of competing against the poverty he hated, Carnegie, influenced by his father's perseverance, became wealthy, successful, and admired. Ironically, the college he left after flunking his Latin course awarded him an honorary degree in 1955, the year of his death. Carnegie said it best in his own words:

"HAPPINESS DOESN'T DEPEND ON ANY EXTERNAL CONDITIONS, IT IS GOVERNED BY OUR MENTAL ATTITUDE."

Every human life illustrates the importance of one's soul. The mind with a persistent belief, as that of Dale Carnegie's, combined with the will to persist against all odds, and a passion to live that belief and communicate it to others, illustrates a soul's growth in process, a person of destiny. There is no possible way to evaluate the importance of our soul or mind, for they are priceless. According to our own estimation of the powers within us, so will we become what we were created to become.

"It is Well with My Soul." Many have sung that well-known hymn, sharing its sentiments, yet possibly not understanding the power of the statement: It is well with my soul. The writer of the hymn was Horatio Spafford, a successful lawyer and businessman in Chicago. He and his wife Anna had five children, but they experienced much tragedy. Their young son died from pneumonia, and that same year much of their property was lost in the great Chicago fire. Eventually, Spafford was able to rebuild a flourishing business.

On November 21, 1873, the French ocean liner Ville du Havre was crossing the Atlantic to Europe with 313 passengers on board. Among them were Mrs. Spafford and their four young daughters. Mr. Spafford planned to meet his family later and remained in Chicago. About four days into the crossing, the ocean liner collided with an iron-hulled Scottish ship. Anna quickly brought her girls to the deck, kneeling there with Annie, Margaret Lee, Bessie, and Tanetta, and prayed that God would spare them if that was His will, or to make them willing to endure whatever awaited them. Within 12 minutes, the Ville du Harve slipped beneath the dark waters of the Atlantic, carrying with it 226 of the passengers, including the four Spafford children.

A sailor who was rowing a small boat over the spot where the ship had sunk, saw a woman floating on a piece of wreckage. It was Mrs. Spafford, who was still alive. He pulled her into the boat and they were picked up by a larger vessel which, nine days later, landed them in Cardiff, Wales. From there she wired her husband a message which began, "Saved alone, what shall I do?" Mr. Spafford later framed the telegram and placed it in his office. Another of the ship's survivors later recalled Anna Spafford saying, "God gave me four daughters. Now they have been taken from me. Someday I will understand why."

Mr. Spafford booked passage on the next available ship and left to join his grieving wife. With the ship about four days out, the captain called Spafford to let him know they were over the place where the children went down. Mr. Spafford returned to his cabin and wrote these words: "When peace like a river attendeth my way, when sorrows like sea billows roll; whatever my lot, Thou hast taught me to say, it is well, it is well with my soul."

From grief, tragedy, and heartbreak, from what someone has called "the dark night of the soul," great and noble truths can emerge, truths that stay within the hearts of thousands or millions who follow. The inner strength, courage, and confidence that could extract such words from the soul of a father at that time, show each of us an idea of the power instilled within us. Strength builds upon strength and such inner strength produces courage. At times when life demands all the strength and courage we can muster, it is profoundly blessed to be able to say "It is well with my soul."

> *"A DARK CLOUD IS NO SIGN THAT THE SUN HAS LOST ITS LIGHT; AND DARK BLACK CONVICTIONS ARE NO ARGUMENTS THAT GOD HAS LAID ASIDE HIS MERCY."*
>
> — CHARLES SPURGEON

CHAPTER 25

Gateways to Purpose and Significance

"EVERY PERSON HAS a longing to be significant, to make a contribution, to be part of something noble and purposeful," said author, speaker, and pastor Dr. John C. Maxwell. At all times when we do the best we can, with what we have, where we are, we position ourselves for the life purpose for which we were created. True as this fact is, we seldom recognize it at the time. Good intentions may seem virtuous but unexciting. And the ordinary day, while pleasurable, often doesn't seem to add to our major accomplishments.

It takes a few decades of life experience for us to realize that nothing in life is unimportant or wasted. Mistakes and failures have value when we learn from them the lessons that become our "practical education." On my website, there is a striking photograph a friend and neighbor in Backus, Minnesota, sent me. It is the image of the gateway to the farm where I spent my youthful years in endless toil and hard labor. There was no gate when our near-destitute family of three moved into the long-abandoned farmhouse. The early spring day in April was bitter cold when a team of four horses pulled our truck and our earthly possessions through deep snow to the empty house that would be my home for the next 13 years.

In this recent photograph, the oak gate that we put up in 1946 stands firmly as it has for the past 71 years. When we set the oak trees that became the gate posts, I remember pouring oil around them as we tamped the soil to make them firm. This simple picture speaks of restoration and achievement. So much happened during the years between my boyhood and the time I turned 25, when I drove through that gate and into the outside world, where I would live and work and establish a profession. Today that picture hangs on my office wall above my desk, as a reminder of the difficult and demanding years that had such a positive influence upon my life and character.

Those years of deprivation and struggle beyond my understanding provided everything I later needed for a life of meaning, accomplishment, and prosperity. That is the good report, but the much better report was that the values and lessons those years instilled in me made me appreciate the future I was destined to live. Frustrated and confused at 15, I asked my beloved mother to explain the purpose of our poverty and struggle and constant unending work. As I have related, my loving mother gave me the best answer she could: "Ask God to show you His purpose for your life." I asked that question in prayer every day, but nothing seemed to change. My work increased and my responsibilities increased, as we slowly made improvements, expanded our efforts, and added more livestock to what became the Triple J Stock Farm. It seemed to me that I was doing nothing more than chopping wood, carrying water, plowing fields, feeding hogs, milking cows, and doing my schoolwork by lamplight in the early hours between 2:00 a.m. and 5:00 a.m., before going to the barn to start those long days all over again. This was my life and the ceaseless labor and battle against hopelessness seemed like a living hell.

Today I appreciate and thank God for my parents who trusted me, depended upon me, and expected the best from me at all times. It was a matter of survival for my seriously ill father, once very active as a successful building contractor, to guide and direct his developing son in doing a man's work and accepting a man's responsibilities. My devoted mother literally kept my father alive by the care she gave him and displayed the character and courage of a pioneer woman. My father demanded absolute integrity and perfection of effort. Slowly I began to see that among the three of us things were improving year by year. My father lived. We did not starve. We had formidable challenges, but we also had inner resources. Each of us, in our own way, became a competent problem solver: a team of three from Hollywood, California, in the wilderness of Northern Minnesota. Anne Sullivan, an American teacher who was best known for being the instructor and lifelong companion of blind and deaf Helen Keller, once said:

"I HAVE THOUGHT ABOUT IT A GREAT DEAL, AND THE MORE I THINK, THE MORE CERTAIN I AM THAT OBEDIENCE IS THE GATEWAY THROUGH WHICH KNOWLEDGE, YES, AND LOVE, TOO, ENTER THE MIND OF THE CHILD."

I vividly remember the day I drove through that gate pictured on my website. I entered the world of opportunity I had hoped for so long. At age 25, when disease destroyed our cattle and all that we had worked to achieve, I was required to venture into the world of business. I had no formal education and no job experience, just the burden of farm debts and the knowledge that I must support my parents. I had to find a way of making a living that would sustain our collective needs. Little could I have imagined that by age 33, all our debts would be repaid, I would have established my own business, and discovered my life's purpose. Everything I needed for all that I accomplished had been instilled in me during the years I lived and worked on the land behind that gate.

Each life has its own gateway, and each of us at some time are confined in a place from which we want to leave, as we look into a world of wonder, potential, and possibility. Some of us enjoy that confinement and security; others long for freedom, adventure, and a chance to prove to ourselves what we are capable of doing. I chose the latter course. My early successes required all of the hard work, sacrifice, and physical labor I once detested, but those successes helped me overcome our indebtedness, and enabled me to purchase the freedom to build my own business, my own future, and to fulfill the purpose for which I had prayed so long.

Very early in my professional life, I conducted my first capital campaign for The Salvation Army, which was the first step in finding that purpose for my life. I had conducted a number of campaigns for other worthy organizations, but this organization was different, and those who worked for it were different. They were dedicated, they were committed, they had a purpose, and it was good. The 4-H public speaking contests during my teen years on the farm had given me awards and personal confidence, and I had a natural talent for business, problem solving, and finance. These elements led me into a 38-year career of guiding community leaders and some of America's greatest CEOs in successful fundraising campaigns, which built and sustained The Salvation Army's facilities and services throughout the southern United States.

The qualities I gained as a boy in small-town Minnesota, those of responsibility, sacrifice, and caring to the extreme for one's neighbor, I saw every day as I worked with Salvationists. It was indescribably gratifying to significantly help the high purpose of these men and women who asked little for themselves, but gave everything to others. As the founder of The Salvation Army, William Booth, once said:

"YOUR DAYS AT THE MOST CANNOT BE VERY LONG, SO USE THEM TO THE BEST OF YOUR ABILITY FOR THE GLORY OF GOD AND THE BENEFIT OF YOUR GENERATION."

My life story, which has been compared to Horatio Alger's rags to riches stories, is similar to thousands of others in America. Most of us believe that success follows hard work and well-meaning efforts. Often this is true, but the fortunate among us discover there is more to life than wealth and achievements.

I think of an ambitious young Texas woman who grew up in a loving, faith-filled home with little money for anything beyond necessities. Like many young women, she dreamed of the life she would enjoy when she grew up. She married early, had a beautiful daughter, and soon after a divorce. The energetic young woman knew she could not afford defeat. She took a job to support herself and continued to dream of the life she wanted. She would marry a successful businessman, she reasoned, and have a happy home, like her parents. Slender, attractive, and possessed of a happy personality, Dee confidently anticipated the day her fairy tale would come true.

It all turned out exactly as she dreamed. Glenn Simmons was a well-respected and very successful businessman. The two fell in love and married and everything Dee ever wanted became possible. She was a wife to be proud of—good looking, well dressed, and intelligent. Soon she established a line of high fashion items, which became so successful that her name was well-known among buyers and fashion magazines. Her energy and dedication never lagged and her husband was proud of his hard-working, successful wife.

After several years of non-stop work, travel, recognition, and success, the fairy tale ended. Glenn came home from a business trip one night in 1987 to learn that his beloved wife had received a breast cancer diagnosis. He assured her they would find the best medical help available, wherever in the world they would need to go. After days of research, the couple discovered the best place for treatment was in their own hometown of Dallas.

The surgery was successful, but the patient's physical recovery was far swifter than the surgery her soul seemed to need. Dee found herself questioning why she had cancer. At that time, she said, "I had a decision to make. Did I want to live, or did I want to die?" Needing answers, Dee returned to her childhood faith. She needed to find purpose for the profound, unexpected loss she suffered. She prayed for answers. One day she discovered a small pamphlet in the kitchen cupboard.

"Nobody knew where it came from, and my kitchen is so well-organized, I can find anything in the dark," she said. There was no explanation for the origin of the brochure filled with nutrition information. Curious about what she read, she dialed the telephone number and spoke at length with a woman who had nutrition information most people at the time hardly bothered to know. She herself had never been concerned with what she ate.

"I could have a dozen chocolate chip cookies with my coffee every morning, and never gained an ounce. My energy was great; I worked far longer than most people, and thought I was healthy." But talking with this woman and her search for purpose in her life, led Dee Simmons to begin an in-depth study of nutrition. With her husband's approval, she made appointments with top research physicians and traveled any distance for interviews and information. She eventually became extremely knowledgeable about how good nutrition was important to a healthy lifestyle.

She said, "Doctors began to call me from around the country, requesting that I talk with patients who were experiencing a cancer crisis of their own." Since she chose not to hide her cancer experience, soon people she did not know were calling for advice. Word got out that she knew how to guide someone else through a cancer experience, and from that day forward Dee Simmons' life took an unprecedented turn. Among all the people she knew, she alone seemed able to give a fearful patient confidence about how to handle this most difficult situation, sustain himself or herself through treatments, and believe in good outcomes. She gave far more than practical advice, however. Often she took phone calls late at night, traveled across town to escort a terrified individual to an oncologist office, record instructions, and even stay at the bedside of someone emerging from surgery.

Nine years after her diagnosis in 1987, Dee started her own nutritional supplements company called Ultimate Living. She had the means to pursue this course and vowed to use only the highest value elements in her products. Today, Dee Simmons has turned over her business to her daughter and works full-time as a patient advocate. The individuals she has counseled, prayed with, and visited number in the hundreds, and her contacts extend as far as Nepal. She can reach leading oncologists anywhere in the world and finds herself counseling both little known and famous people. "There is a New York CEO who phoned me recently and a well-known pastor whose name you would recognize," she said. "Sickness happens to everyone and cancer is complicated. I am available at any hour, seven days a week."

From an all-too-common personal tragedy, Dee Simmons found a life's purpose that far transcends the ideas she held as an ambitious young woman. Her Cinderella marriage enabled both partners to find far more meaning than their first exciting romance. From the indulged and adored wife, Dee grew into a woman of formidable resources and great heart. Beyond her first dreams of success and substance, she knows the true significance of all lives, as well as her own. As Roy T. Bennett, the author of *The Light in the Heart* wrote:

> **"LEARN TO LIGHT A CANDLE IN THE DARKEST MOMENTS OF SOMEONE'S LIFE. BE THE LIGHT THAT HELPS OTHERS SEE; IT IS WHAT GIVES LIFE ITS DEEPEST SIGNIFICANCE."**

We often fail to recognize the significance of ordinary actions or decisions at the time. As I look at our farm's gate posts, recalling the day we cut the two trees and dragged them out of the woods, I think of how much work it took and how my father required it be done. They had to be sawed, cut to proper size, and the bark had to be removed. The process was tedious and took several days. It took a full day to dig the post holes which were partially filled with crankcase oil to preserve the wood. The neighbor brought his truck with a log-lifting crane to raise each tree and put it into the post hole. Each time I look at that picture, I think of my father and the lessons he taught me. Nearly seven decades later, those posts remain standing because of the way they were made. At the time, it seemed an unrewarding job that I was glad to have finished. But we cannot begin to measure the effects of the jobs we do, how long they will remain, or what effect they will have on the lives of others. Those gateposts are far sturdier than the young man I believed myself to be at the time they were set.

Ross Mason, a highly successful Atlanta businessman, was 37 when his life abruptly changed. While training for the New Zealand Ironman Triathlon, he was riding a bicycle on the Silver Comet Trail when he says, "I saw a bee fly into my helmet and instinctively knew it would sting me. Unfortunately, when it stung me, I jerked my handlebars in reaction to the bee sting and lost control of my bike. When I came to, I was laying on the ground with a tree branch in my face and I was unable to move it."

Ross remained calm, even as he realized he could not move his legs. In the ambulance, he felt at peace and actually joked with the EMS personnel. They questioned him on why he was so calm, considering what had just happened to him. Ross informed them he was a Christian and was not afraid of death. No matter what happened, he knew he would be all right.

Early in his rehabilitation, a therapist asked Ross to try and write his ABCs. He remembers his frustration: "It was so disheartening for me to be given a crayon and told to write my ABCs. Give me something meaningful that I can do in the process of my recovery. Let me reach out to a wounded soldier, or help a nonprofit serving widows and orphans. Let me learn to write again that way. Don't ask me to write my ABCs! Don't just check off a box. Help me to regain my dignity, to recover spiritually, socially, and emotionally, not just physically."

Ross has never stopped since his accident. This man of action clearly has won his own Ironman Triathlon, as his life reaches further and further beyond his wheelchair. He visualizes a global innovation campus, now being planned, that will lead the world in collaborative research, innovation, and transformation in healthcare. In 2004, he founded a venture philanthropy before his accident that, ironically, was initially focused on neurorecovery. It is now focused on connecting innovators to sources of capital, strategic partners, technology solutions, and servant leaders so that together they are more effective at saving lives, saving money, and having a sustainable impact. To learn more about Ross' organization called HINRI - The Healthcare Institute for National Renewal and Innovation, visit www.hinri.org.

Today, Ross recounts countless miracles dating back to his childhood. In Ross' own words, "There have been many, many miracles occurring in my life over the past several months and years. One of the most recent and exciting miracles has been my own physical healing. In 2013, I met Ron Burhoff, who has an amazing prophetic and healing gift from God. On November 24, 2013, he confirmed God's calling on my life and prophesied that I would be completely healed. I have a "complete" C-6 spinal cord injury, which means I should never have any sensation or function below my collar bones. I woke up the very next morning after praying with Ron and God had completely restored my lungs and diaphragm, as well as many of my back and stomach muscles. I was also able to press 65 pounds with my legs for the first time in 7 years. I met with my doctor a month later and he was literally weeping over the miracle of my physical recovery. I believe Matthew 11:1-6 and I know that God has completely healed me and it is now just a question of manifesting itself in my body. Many of my friends, caregivers, nurses, and even strangers have had dreams about my complete and total recovery. I am very excited about getting out of the wheelchair and engaging once again in a very active life."

While he waits for physical miracles to manifest, he proclaims miracles of every other sort in his life and the lives of others. Ross lives in a large house where he offers genuine hospitality for businessmen and travelers. He gives generously of his information, advice, and time to many people, and lives what some might consider a handicapped life far beyond such boundaries. At age 47, as this is written, Ross Mason's work and influence has spanned the globe. He may never know if his triumphs are because of his tragedy or in spite of it. Those who know him consider his life's work and faith to be immensely significant.

Beyond our desires for success and substance, the adventurous soul envisions the sort of meaningful missions Ross Mason suggested. The creative mind searches for more than the eye can see. I recall my neighbor, who sent me the picture of my farm gate. The picture is beautiful. My life within that gate was so hopeless and seemingly so meaningless that it was 25 years before I could bring myself to return to the farm and walk the dirt road I had walked so many times when I was a boy struggling to become a man. By that time, my family and I were well-established in Little Rock, Arkansas, happy and healthy, my father still alive. Eventually I would deed that beautiful farmland on Pine Mountain Lake to

The Salvation Army for use as a youth camp, in memory of my parents. Now I consider the image of the gate through which I thought I had escaped and realize I never really left. That place, that small town of Backus, those wonderful neighbors, taught me fundamental life principles that helped me become a man worthy of my manhood.

The neighbor I mentioned, a wonderful, intelligent young woman, confided to me about her passion for teaching. She longed to achieve a master's degree in education and I was pleased to help her find scholarship funds. To my joy and appreciation, she earned that degree and today serves as a school principal. I look at her photo of my gateway and realize it led somehow into her life, with her life bringing untold significance into the lives of hundreds of boys and girls. In that way, my small contribution and interest in her future will extend untold significance possibly through generations.

Abraham Lincoln once said that:

"GOD MUST LOVE THE COMMON MAN, SINCE HE MADE SO MANY OF THEM."

There really are no common, ordinary people, but there are countless ordinary lives. The person we believe to be ordinary is equipped for significance far beyond anything they can imagine. I believe that each person created by the Father of all fathers is designed to reflect the divine purpose for which they were born. Despite the circumstances of our birth or heritage, each of us comes equipped for more than we can imagine.

Our life is a matter of choice. We can desire success and substance and achieve both, often without too much trouble. The truth is, even the least of us is able to go far beyond a materialistic lifestyle into one of giving, of gratitude, of service, and of significance. The American author H.P. Lovecraft once said:

"WHAT A MAN DOES FOR PAY IS OF LITTLE SIGNIFICANCE. WHAT HE IS, AS A SENSITIVE INSTRUMENT RESPONSIVE TO THE WORLD'S BEAUTY, IS EVERYTHING!"

At all times, we are choosing the better way as we do the best we can, with what we have, where we are, at all times. You are not an ordinary person. You can be what you desire to be, if you will do your best with what you have in mind, body, and spirit. What does your life portray?

> *"WHEN WE TALK ABOUT HAVING A LIFE OF SIGNIFICANCE AND MEANING, IT'S NOT ABOUT FAME OR MONEY OR RESOURCES. IT'S ABOUT PEOPLE AND LIVES AND HEARTS. THAT'S MY BIGGEST PASSION IN LIFE."*
>
> —Tim Tebow
> METS Baseball Player

CHAPTER 26

A Walk with an Older Man

I TOOK A walk one day with an older man, a man much older than me. While we walked he shared some thoughts that I will share with you. He told me of the lessons he'd learned and the way life seemed to work. He said life had its ups and downs and we all have challenges that we must face. He said we shouldn't measure our life by the years we live, but by the way we live our years. Some folks are old when they are young and others young when they are old; it all depends upon how they think and what their thoughts represent.

He told me that the more I learned, the more I would find there was to learn. To him life was a journey we travel from birth to death. He said that life was like an endless circle for those who see the tides of life as they ebb and flow. To him life was a reflection of our thoughts, and what we see in others was a reflection of what we see in ourselves. Our life is an expression of our soul's earthly journey, as we travel the road that leads to our earthly destination, and return to the source from whence we came. The beginning is found in the ending and the ending is found in the beginning. Life begets life and hope begets hope as we become the result of what has been.

As we walked together I thought of what he said and how we live beyond our own life. I couldn't tell how old he was for his steps were firm and his thoughts seemed to travel far beyond what I could see or understand. He seemed to see what was to come long before it came to be. He would explain to me how his experience gave vision to his thoughts.

My mind was filled with thoughts that revolved around me and the things I desired and wanted to possess. I heard what he was saying when he spoke of me, and how fine my life could be if I would do my best. He said life was full of opportunities for those who really tried, and I could have what I desired if I would do my best. The more he spoke of what I could be, the bigger I became, until he said life had its price and the price was often high. When I questioned what he meant by the price of life, he asked what I was willing to pay for the life I desired to live. As he told me of the price I would be required to pay, I began to wonder how such a price was ever to be paid. He said I could have it all if I would pay the price: the same price he had paid for the life that he had lived. He said that nothing in life was ever free from cost, that all things had their price, and for some the price was great.

He said we must think in terms of value for all that we desire, and in the years to come, all of our desires would bear their own fruit. I soon realized that the man with whom I walked would become my teacher and my mentor. He was not a scholar and the lessons he had learned were the lessons that no school had ever taught. I found to my surprise that he was a simple man who spoke in simple terms and used examples more than words. He made me feel secure because he gave me confidence and he never spoke of faults or failures or other weaknesses. He spoke of many things and conditions that I had never considered. His words and thoughts opened a new world to me as my life came into view.

He spoke of creative thoughts and the power of our mind, and explained how spiritual strength gave meaning to our life. He told me that prayer had been the source of his achievements and the power behind the purpose that motivated what he did. As we looked down the road on which we were walking, he explained how a man could live beyond himself, and how we each have the need to live beyond our time and a purpose beyond ourselves.

He spoke of immortality and how this is achieved by the way we live for others until our life has ended. We achieve lasting life by the good we do and the good we share with others. Our good efforts and encouragement will give a worthy life to our deeds and our creeds. These were stimulating thoughts as I became aware that I would not be the same person that I had been before. My mind was filled with visions of the man that I could be, if I was willing to pay the price that life would ask of me.

As I think of the ways my life has changed since we first met, I see how God fulfills our needs through the people that we meet. We know not when they will appear or the form they will take, for it is God who brings them to us at our time of greatest need. His words were often spoken in the form of a request when he asked me what I desired to be and wanted most from life. He reminded me again that my desires would have their price and the coin of life that I would use would never be in cash. He said the price is paid in "self and substance" for that which we desire: in qualities of character, integrity, consistency of efforts, and nobility of intentions. These are the coins of payment for the life we desire to live.

He said that if I hoped to be a man worthy of my desires I must live my life to the fullest of my ability and do my best at whatever I did. He made me think in ways that I had never thought before. My mind was being challenged and my world was not the same. He challenged me to think of what I could do with what I had, as he gave me answers to the questions that I asked. What I learned from him enriched my life as he would share truths with me that I could understand. He told me that life had more to offer than most people believed, because their faith in themselves was limited by the doubts that they perceived.

He spoke of some of the qualities I should work to acquire, qualities I could not purchase with money because they must be earned by effort to be possessed. He spoke of those people and things in a person's life that never lose their value, because their value relates to the qualities that make life worth living. He believed that a person's true worth was found in their attitude and the qualities revealed through their character. He believed that those who live for themselves live an empty and lonely life, for they give sparingly and seek to live abundantly. He believed that to have we must give and to live we must share.

Such thoughts as these encouraged me to think beyond myself and try to understand what lies beyond me and my desires. He told me that our life was a reflection of our thoughts, and the longer we lived the more we became the reflection of our thoughts. He took the time to explain the conceptions he had shared, for some were far beyond my understanding until he made them clear. He said life was like a circle; we become what we have been for we are constantly evolving from the person we were to the person we are. He said young life begets older life and older gives way to younger life. The flow of life evolves from what has been to what will be. As the seed creates the plant, the plant creates the seed. Like begets like as the thought is the seed of the act it creates.

We know not from where we came nor do we know where we will go. Our time of coming was before our birth and our going is beyond our death. Life is like a drop of water drawn by the sun from the sea from which it came and will return again as fallen rain. It will rise again and again to the heavens from which it came, as our soul came to us at birth and will return again to its source. The circle of life continues as we live on in the lives of others: the lives of those our life has touched by our love and understanding.

He spoke of the endless life of giving, and how what we give lives on in the lives of those our life has touched, as a seed that we have planted grows in the soil of other lives. Our deeds and words become the seeds we plant in the soil of other lives, and in those lives we will live when our time on earth is over. He said our soul came to us complete and will leave us as it came and return to the source from whence it came, for in the life of God there is no end.

It was his belief that our spirit is the power within us, and our soul and mind are bound together by our faith and our commitment. As I listened to the words he spoke, I began to understand the qualities of life that mattered most to those who saw beyond themselves. He said that a man's good name was a reflection of his life, and I should strive throughout my life to be worthy of my good name.

I am older now than I was when our walk began, and the memory of that walk has guided my life. I am wiser now and understand that with God's help, I've become more of the man I was created to be. I thank God there are those who will take the time to share their experience and love with others.

> *"AND IT SHALL COME TO PASS AFTERWARD THAT I WILL POUR OUT MY SPIRIT UPON ALL FLESH; AND YOUR SONS AND YOUR DAUGHTERS SHALL PROPHESY, YOUR OLD MEN SHALL DREAM DREAMS, YOUR YOUNG MEN SHALL SEE VISIONS."*
>
> *—JOEL 2:28 (KJV)*

About the Author

Jack C. McDowell, business leader, philanthropist, author, and public speaker, was born in Hollywood, California, during the Great Depression and reared on a farm in Backus, Minnesota. For 38 years he served as The Salvation Army's Management Counsel for the Southern United States. He has led more than 100 successful capital campaigns to serve and expand the work of The Salvation Army. In addition he has conducted many successful capital campaigns for churches, colleges, synagogues, and schools.

In 1995, he donated his Triple J Stock Farm in Backus, Minnesota, to The Salvation Army for a Youth Camp, in memory of his parents. In 2005, the author endowed The Salvation Army's Jack McDowell School for Leadership Development in Atlanta, Georgia. He has now fulfilled the material commitments he made when he wrote his Life Plan. He has authored three other books: *There's more to Life than Making a Living*, *The Power of Purpose*, and *Hope, Desire, and Aspire*.

His 50 years of marriage to Peggy Weber of Salzburg, Austria, joined two highly successful business careers as each supported and encouraged the other. Peggy's family candle-making business was established in 1583. Her combined artistry and business efforts created Emperor Art Creations, through which she distributed her European-designed candles in America. The McDowell's contribute substantially to philanthropic and cultural institutions in both countries. They reside in Atlanta, Georgia, and Salzburg, Austria.

www.ingramcontent.com/pod-product-compliance
Lightning Source LLC
Chambersburg PA
CBHW070638050426
42451CB00008B/207